Palmistry for All

Be your own pal
line, sign, and mark
hidden potential an
character, draw on your best options, and chart out your life to your advantage.

Copiously illustrated, *Palmistry for All* has an appeal for each reader. Its hallmark lies in its simple and systematic explanation and interpretation of the prominent and not-so prominent features of the hand, their permutations and combinations, and their effect on the individual.

The author, Pandit Ashutosh Ojha, is a well-known palmist and astrologer. He has a number of books on different aspects of palmistry to his credit; this is one of the more popular ones.

". . . will stimulate interest, both of scoffers and enthusiasts. Those who are genuinely interested in what their lines foretell will find the book very much worth their perusal."

Tribune

"A scientifically written and well-illustrated book on palmistry."

M.P. Chronicle

By the Same Author
in
Orient Paperbacks

Numerology for All

PALMISTRY FOR ALL

Pt. Ashutosh Ojha

Orient Paperbacks

DELHI | MUMBAI | HYDERABAD

www.orientpaperbacks.com

ISBN 13: 978-81-222-0120-8
ISBN 10: 81-222-0120-2

1st Published 1972
9th Revised & Enlarged Edition 1995
15th Printing 2005

Palmistry for All

Cover design by Vision Studio

Published by
Orient Paperbacks
(A division of Vision Books Pvt. Ltd.)
5A/8 Ansari Road, New Delhi-110 002

Printed in India at
Jay Kay Offset Printers, Delhi-110 041

Cover Printed at
Ravindra Printing Press, Delhi-110 006

Contents

1

Introduction

The lines of the palm, the shape and structure of the hand, the detailed markings such as islands, forks, grilles, and cross-bars—have all been studied in their variety of combinations by palmists through the years. There is sufficient evidence to show that fortune-telling through palmistry was practised in most ancient civilizations. Some people believe that it was first practised in China over five thousand years ago. Others opine that Egypt or India can claim to be the first protagonist of palmistry. References to palmistry have been found in the Sanskrit epics of the pre-Christian era. The gypsies, who are known for palm-reading, originally inhabited India and later migrated to different parts of the world, thereby spreading their knowledge far and wide. It is to the ancient Greeks, however, that the credit goes for a comprehensive presentation of the study.

It was from the Greek word cheir'—the hand—that palmistry unfolded into two branches: Chirognomy, which endeavours to analyse the psychological and emotional make-up of a person through the shape of his hand, and Chiromancy, which foretells a person's future by interpreting the lines of his hand.

The first datable use of the word 'palmistry' was found in a book written in English in the fifteenth century, though it was, perhaps, in use far earlier on. The nineteenth century witnessed a definite revival in the popularity of the subject, defying earlier attempts to brand it as superstition, speculative prognostication or even, mere fantasy.

Of late, sceptics, scientists, and men of learning have come to believe and accept that there is certainly a connection between palmistry and the individual, and his destiny. They are increasingly being convinced that palmistry is not just an entertaining topic of drawing-room discussion or an interesting pastime. It is a guide towards understanding the virtues and vices, the mental traits, and propensities of persons one comes in contact with.

Palmistry is, indeed, a mirror of your own character. When a palmist gives you an accurate description of 'yourself', you are able to verify the views you have of yourself or modify them, or then, face some hard truths about yourself. The fact that the palm-reader is able to make a thorough reading, merely from the lines of your palm print and not from any previously provided data, can unnerve even the staunchest critic of palmistry. Another convincing argument in favour of palmistry is that when finger prints are used to detect criminals, palm prints too must surely offer distinctive and unique information about the individual.

Many medical doctors concede that since the human hand is a dominant example of the advanced stage of development of man, the lines on the palm reflect the physiological workings of the brain. Aristotle acknowledged the superiority of the hand as 'the organ of organs'. However, just as no two personalities are identical, no two hands are alike — not even those of identical twins!

Reading the hand is a study that requires painstaking effort and patience. Like any art, it cannot be mastered in a day. Hands which may once have all looked the same, will gradually 'come alive!' A word of caution though! It is not generally a good idea to practise palm-reading on yourself. Since we all have some preconceived notions about ourselves, our reading should be coloured by these thoughts. It is far better to study other palms to develop clarity of thought and accuracy of interpretation.

A question commonly asked is: Which hand should be examined for reading—right or left? Old Indian tradition attached more importance to the right hand of males and the left hand of females. Later palmists espoused the belief that 'the left is the hand we are born with; the right is the hand we make.' In other words, the left hand indicates the qualities and characteristics we are born with; and the right hand denotes what we make of our life, based on our environment, experiences, and influences. However, modern-day palm readers examine and compare both hands simultaneously. After comparing the differences, they concentrate on the hand more frequently used by the subject (right hand for right-handed people, left hand for left-handed), since that is the hand which carries out the orders of the brain. Therefore, the development of lines on that hand are what will provide an insight into the future.

Right through your voyage of discovery, look at the hand as a whole first; then integrate the details. A single marking or sign is only a piece of the jigsaw; it must be put in context with all the other features of the hand. This is the key towards making an authentic and irrefutable interpretation.

2

The Shape of the Hand

The shape of the hand has always intrigued palmists. The hand is a living marvel which expresses a gamut of emotions—joy, sorrow, penitence, hesitation, and so on. It demands, summons, promises, and denies. It can arouse a mob and placate an agitated crowd. No two hands are alike—not even those of identical twins! Beautiful hands often lack a strong personality, while squarish, knotty, or stubby hands often belie an artistic and philosophical nature.

There is generally a tendency among beginners to neglect the study of the shape of the hand, the quality of the fingers, the texture of the skin, the position of the thumb, and the overall consideration which should be given to these features. They proceed directly to the study of lines on the palm and any marks found thereon. A little forethought will show that this is not the right course, for the effect of the lines and the marks on the palm have to be evaluated against the background of the type of hand which is being studied.

Let us first give some general information about the hand.

General Features

Size of the Hand: The size of the hand is generally in

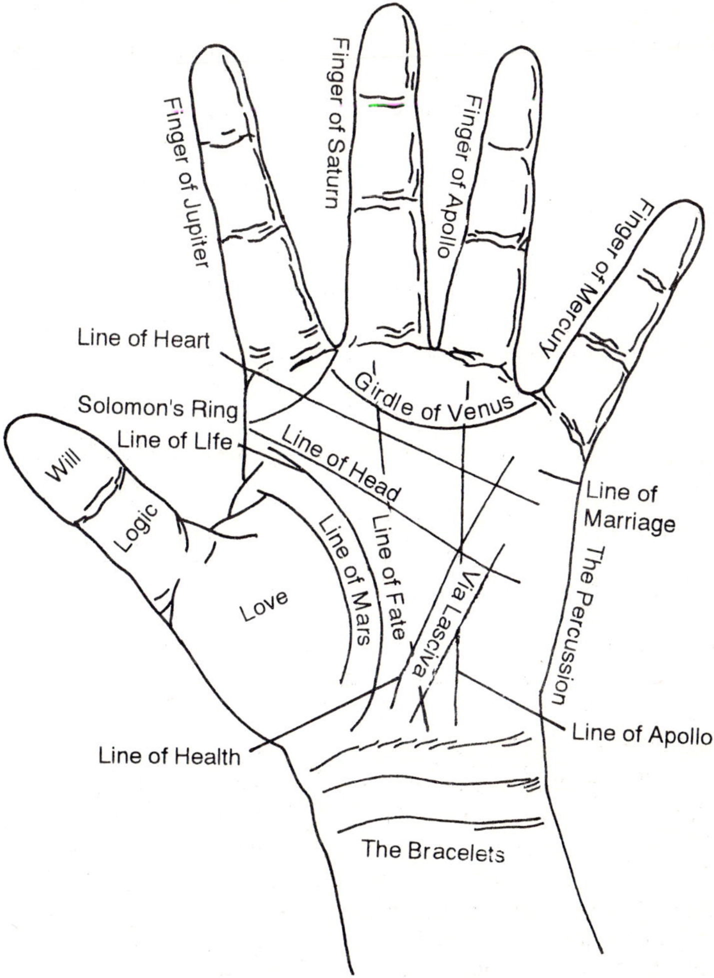

Fig 1 The Shape of the Hand

proportion to the size of the body, but sometimes we come across people of the same height and built having different sizes of hands. When the size of the hand is larger than average, it is called a large hand; when the size is less than average, it is called a small hand.

When the length of the hand, commencing from the bracelets (Fig.1) to the tip of the middle finger, is proportionately longer, it is called a long hand. When it is smaller, it is called a small hand. When the width of the palm from the root of the thumb to the percussion (see Fig.1) is proportionately more, it is called a broad hand.

The Two Sides of the Hand: The side on which there are lines on the palm is called the 'inside'; the reverse side on which there is hair on men's hands particularly, is called the 'back' of the hand.

Texture of the Skin: An unblemished and smooth skin shows refinement; a coarse skin indicates vulgarity. If the hand is unduly soft and the skin is also smooth, the individual is likely to be lazy.

Hair: Hair is generally found on the back of men's hands. It is also found on the second knuckles and, in some hands, on the first knuckles too. If a man has no hair on the back of his hand, it indicates a lack of virility and effiminacy of character. If the growth of hair is thick and excessive, it indicates coarseness and cruelty. Ladies, generally, do not have hair on the back of their hand. If they do, the lady in question could be considered manly and a virago.

Shape of the Fingers and the Palm: The 'palm proper' extends from the bracelet to the root of the middle finger. If the middle finger comprises about three-fourths of the palm proper, the size of the fingers should be treated as normal. If the middle finger is longer than three-fourths of the palm proper, the fingers should be treated as long. If it is shorter than the normal length, they should be treated as short.

Similarly, if the palm is longer in proportion than as discussed above, it is called a *lcng palm.* If it is shorter than the above-mentioned proportion, it is called a *short palm.*

When both the sides of the palm bulge far beyond the width of the four fingers, it is called a *broad palm.* If it is of the same width as that of the four fingers, it is normal. If it is narrower, it is called a *narrow palm.*

When you open the hand, the side towards the fingers is referred to as the *upper side,* and the portion of the palm towards the wrist is described as the *lower side.* If the Line of Heart is not in the normal position on the palm, and runs through the upper portion of the palm, it is said to be 'high'. But if it passes through the lower portion of the palm, it is called 'low' or 'downwards'. The phrases 'high and low' or 'upper and lower' are used to describe the location.

Having acquainted ourselves with some terms used in palmistry, we shall now deal with various types of hands.

Types of Hands

Ancient palmists have divided the hand into seven types. They are being dealt individually in the following paragraphs.

The Elementary Hand: An unrefined hand, with small thick fingers, short nails, a broad and thick palm, clumsy in appearance, and having only three main lines (of Life, Head and Heart) is called an *elementary hand.*

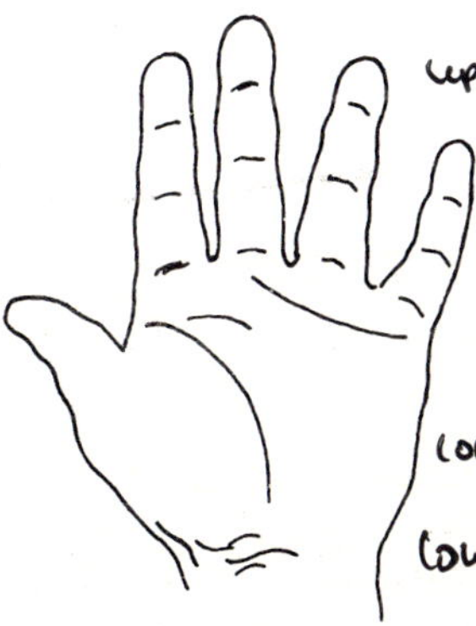

Fig 2 Elementary Hand

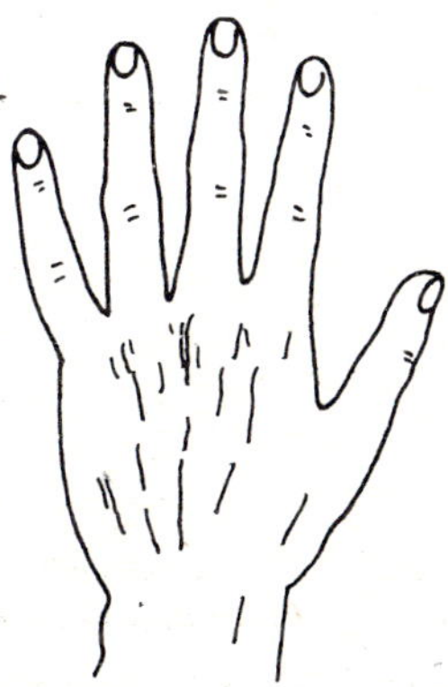

Fig 3 Conic Hand

In such a hand, the Line of Head is generally short. This is considered to be the lowest type of hand.

Conic Hand: The *conic hand* is neither large nor small. It is of medium size and is generally soft (Fig. 3). The fingers are tapering at the end. They are not so pointed as in the philosophic hand; they are semi-pointed. The nails are rather long. Some palmists also call this the artist's hand because persons with this type of hand are inclined towards the field of arts such as singing, acting, and painting. Since the tips of the fingers are conical in shape, it is called the conic hand.

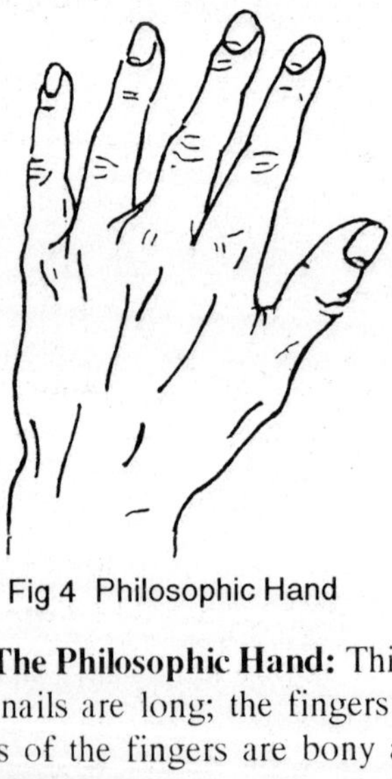

Fig 4 Philosophic Hand

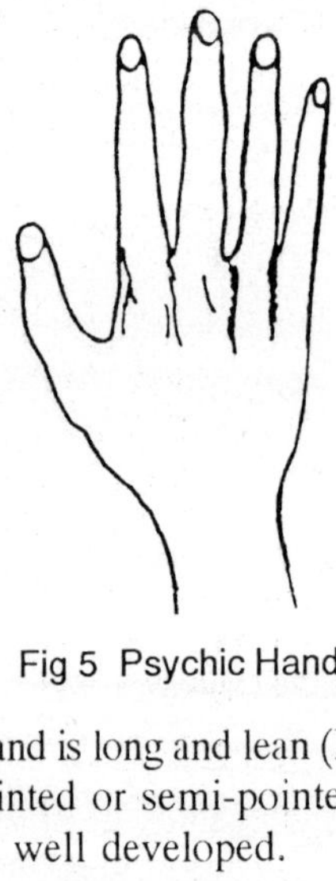

Fig 5 Psychic Hand

The Philosophic Hand: This hand is long and lean (Fig. 4). The nails are long; the fingers pointed or semi-pointed. The knots of the fingers are bony and well developed.

The Psychic Hand: This hand is lean and thin (Fig. 5). It is attractive and delicate in appearance. The fingers are slender and tapering. The nails are oblong.

The Spatulate Hand: When the first phalange of fingers (the nail phalanges) is spread out, it appears wide like a spatula and the hand with such fingers is called a *spatulate hand* (Fig. 6). The palm is also wider at the base of the fingers or at the wrist.

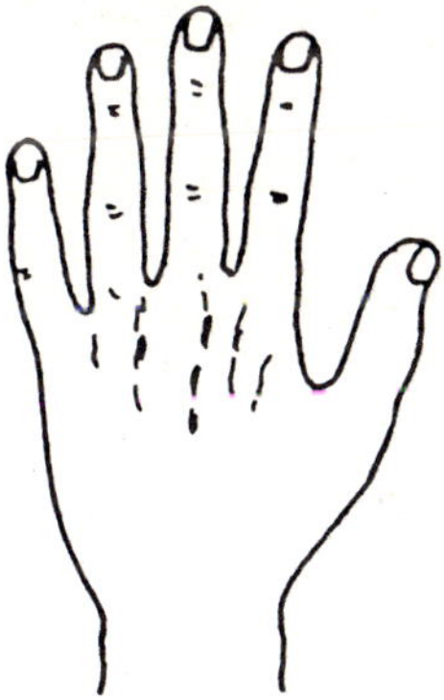

Fig 6 Spatulate Hand

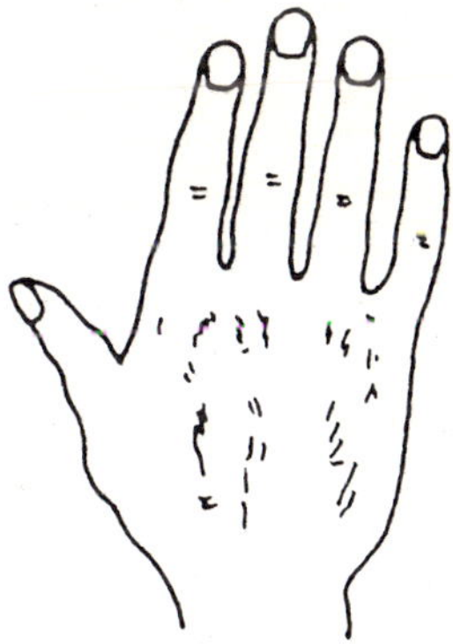

Fig 7 Square Hand

Square Hand: In a *square hand* the length and the breadth of the palm (excluding the fingers) are more or less equal (Fig. 7). The fingers at the tips are neither too broad nor conical.

The Mixed Hand: So far, we have looked at six types of hands: artistic or conic, psychic, philosophic, spatulate, square, and elementary. When the hand is not purely of any of the above types but presents mixed traits of several types, it is called a *mixed hand.*

Characteristics of Different Hands

If you are examining an *elementary hand* comprising a thick and heavy palm—coarse in touch and clumsy in appearance, short fingers, and a thumb with its first phalange being heavy or clubbed (of the shape of a club), can you expect any fineness or intellectuality in the person possessing it! On the contrary, an individual with an elementary hand may be possessed of much animal passion and may even use brute force if his anger is aroused.

Or take the example of a *philosophical hand* which is generally long. This hand is more bony than fleshy. The fingers are long and tapering. They have well developed joints. The nails are long and oblong. Persons with such hands are intellectually sensitive and thoughtful, learned, and lovers of mysticism. But such persons lack the knack for earning money or accumulating wealth. They have little passion for worldly goods. Even a good line of wealth on such a palm would not bear much meaning for the subject. Such hands do not accumulate much wealth. In fact a shorter line of wealth on a square hand would bring in more money than a longer line of wealth on a philosophical or psychic hand.

Like the possessors of a philosophic hand, those who have a *psychic hand* are not practical in outlook, and lack the ability to put in much physical or mental effort. To earn money is against their temperament. The psychic hand is very beautiful. The hand is long and narrow and appears very delicate. It has thin fingers which taper at the end (nail phalanges). The nails are oblong as in a philosophic hand, but they are smaller. There are very few persons who possess purely psychic type of hands. They are more visionary than practical. They are not at all businesslike, and lack punctuality and precision. Colours and sweet melodies of music appeal to them more than day-to-day affairs. They belong to the land of dreams and not to the matter-of-fact world. They possess keen powers of intuition. They are essentially religious, though the rituals of religion appeal to them more than the basic tenets underlying the religion. They are calm and cold.

Such persons do not respond to riches and honours. They may be a good media for hypnotism and may excel others in that field. The Line of Head in such hands will show more imagination than the practical wisdom of the square hand.

There are, however, certain distinguishable features which can make recognition easier. The philosophical hand is large and well developed; the psychic hand is small and slender. The former is bony; the latter is not. In the philosophical hand, the thumb is large; in the psychic hand, it is not so. In the former, the fingers are long with both the joints being markedly knotty; in the latter, the fingers are smooth and the nails are narrower.

The *conic hand* is so called because the fingers taper slightly (become gradually thinner) at the end (nail phalanges). They are full at the base and resemble a cone at the tips. The hand is of medium size, neither as big as the philosophical hand, nor as small as the psychic one.

People with conic hands act more on impulse and instinct than on logic and reason. They are quick and clever in their ideas, but lack in a continuous application of energy and perseverance in executing them. They are persons of strong likes and dislikes. They have an artistic bent of mind, but this faculty in them expresses itself more as a mere appreciation for the arts (all that is beautiful appeals to their eyes, ears and other senses) than any artistic ability. Their temper is quickly aroused but does not last long.

Those who possess a *square-shaped hand* are the most practical people from the worldly point of view. Persons with square hands are endowed with strong common sense; they achieve their objectives and success by dint of hard labour and perseverance. They personify the proverb: Success in life is ninety-nine percent perspiration and one percent inspiration.

If the square hand has short square fingers, then the practical outlook is intensified, and the possessors of such hands become all the more materialistic, and, therefore, plodding. But if the square hand has long square fingers, it indicates a greater development of the mental faculties, and the person possessing it will have more ideas of his own which he will execute successfully. People with longer fingers have sharper logical and reasoning faculties than those with shorter ones. If the fingers in the square hands, besides being long, are also knotty, then the possessors of such hands take into consideration the pros and cons of every matter before going into it.

If the square hand has psychic fingers, much of the utility and practicality would be destroyed. Persons with such hands may commence a piece of work with much practical wisdom, but will leave the same in the middle, unfinished, due to want of application and perseverance.

The square hand with a conic palm may bring success in art, music, and similar fields. But if there are spatulate fingers in a square palm, the combined characteristics may inspire the individual towards practical inventions, i.e. invention of utilitarian goods and articles for household purposes.

And last, but not the least, we come to the *spatulate hand*, that is, the hand which is broader on one side and narrower on the other. If the width of the palm at the base of the fingers is wider and that at the wrist is narrower, the palm will be described as a spatulate palm; if the width of the palm at the base of the fingers is narrower than the width of the palm at the wrist side, then also the palm will be spatulate. For a hand to be called a purely spatulate type of hand, the tips of the fingers should also be spatulate.

If the width of the palm at the base of the fingers is wider than at the wrist, the person is more practical than in the latter type described above.

There are characteristics of the spatulate hand which apply to both types.

When the hand is firm and hard, the person is energetic and enthusiastic, but rather excitable. His industry and application to work are continuous and he accomplishes it. But if the hand is flabby and soft, the person will lack in perseverance. Persons with spatulate hands love independence and have an inventive genius. They generally have large and capable hands. The fingers are long and well developed. Such persons like to execute new ideas and dislike following the beaten track. They are people of action. But due to their extremely independent outlook, their temperament is not very amiable.

Even though the six types of hands have been described above, when we actually examine the hands of people—our friends, acquaintances, or clients—we rarely come across a hand possessing all the characteristics of one type. We mostly come across hands possessing some characteristics of one type and some of the other types. Such hands are called *mixed hands*. Sometimes the shape of the hand may conform to one type, the palm to another, and the fingers to others. All the four fingers also may not be of one type. They may be of one, two or more types. In all such cases, while reading the palm, it is important to assess how many characteristics of which type are in a certain measure and the prominence of their role in the subject's life. You will have to synthesise the influences and then come to a conclusion.

While studying the shape of the hand, we must make a distinction between the hand of a man and that of a woman. The hands of ladies are smaller and more refined. They have more supple muscles and, therefore, many of the qualities pertaining to the square and spatulate types which would be fulfilled in men's hands, will be found in lesser measure in a woman's hand. But, on the other hand, in hands of the psychic type—a woman may be more psychic due to her being more emotional, sensitive, and intuitive.

Sometimes we come across the hand of a congenital idiot. The palm is generally thin and long, so soft that if you squeeze it in your hand or probe the palm with your finger, it will yield no resistance. The weak muscles point to a weak brain. The fingers are smooth and small.

It is not the shape of the hand alone but other characteristics in the hand also which have to be considered before arriving at any conclusion. For example, due importance should be attached to the fingers—their length, smoothness, etc.—for the characteristics of the different types of fingers indicate a variance in personality traits, which we shall deal with in the chapter on fingers. If the fingers support the inferences drawn from the lines and marks in the hand, the predictions will match the events. But if the fingers indicate something contrary to what the line or lines in the palm signify, the ultimate results will not be the same as predicted by the lines and marks on the hand.

This brings us to the influence of the lines and mounts (which are discussed in detail in Chapters 3, 4, and 5). If the Line of Head in a hand is long and fine, then intellectuality is indicated. But if the Mount of Mercury is depleted and low, and the fourth finger weak and deficient, then the owner of the hand will lack in expression, and however well-read he may be, he will not be able to become an author of books. It is necessary to have the strong influence of Mercury to be endowed with the power of expression, either as a lecturer or as an author.

Fingers and mounts are correlated. There are four fingers to four mounts, one for each. The Mounts of Mars and Moon have no fingers presiding over them. And though the thumb is above the Mount of Venus, it does not preside over Venusian qualities. So only the Mounts of Mercury, Apollo, Saturn and Jupiter have fingers presiding over them. The readers would do well to bear in mind that the finger corresponds to the mount at its base, in as much as the two together endow the person with the qualities of the mount. For example, if the Mount of Jupiter is weak, it will be made up in some measure if the Jupiter finger is well formed, erect, and strong.

The converse is also true. If you want to ascertain the Mercurian qualities, and if the Mercury finger is short, feeble and weak, the deficiency caused by it may be made up in some measure by a good Mount of Mercury.

A mention has been made of the influence of the fingers, lines and mounts to impress upon the reader that an inference should be drawn only after an assessment of the hand as a whole and not piecemeal from the various indications.

Generally the shapes of hands and fingertips in one hand of an individual conform to those of the other hand; but sometimes there are noticeable differences in lines and marks.

The most appropriate method of studying palmistry would, therefore, be to examine both hands side by side as explained in the Introduction. It will then be possible to compare an individual's inborn characteristics with the changes that are taking place in his life and predict the future based upon these observations.

3

The Thumb

The palm consists of the thumb, fingers, and the palm. The thumb has been used by anthropologists to study the evolution of man. It is more important than any of the fingers due to its flexibility and is, therefore, a window on understanding the working of the brain.

The thumb has to be studied in respect of its position on the palm; its length and formation; stiffness or suppleness; the proportionate length of the two phalanges; the shape of the first phalange; the shape of the second phalange, and marks on the inner side of the thumb.

Position of the Thumb

The thumb may be set high or low on the palm. 'High' means higher up nearer the base of the first finger; 'low' means lower down towards the base of the palm. If the thumb is high, it indicates a lack of adaptability and miserliness. If it is low, it indicates intelligence and generosity in spending money. If it is neither high nor low, then a mean value of the qualities of high-set and low-set would be signified. If the thumb is small, ill-shaped, and set too high, then the person utterly lacks in brain power. When you stretch out the thumb completely and the thumb makes a right angle or an obtuse angle at its junction with the palm, it indicates an uncommonly independent spirit. The person is aggressive and indomitable, particularly, if the thumb is large in size and the first phalange is strong. If the thumb, when stretched out, makes an acute angle at its base with the palm, then the person lacks an independent mind, particularly, if the thumb is small and the first phalange is weak.

Formation of the Thumb

A long thumb indicates a good capacity to think and execute ideas. An extra long thumb indicates a person who takes decisions according to the dictates of his brain—feelings and emotions do not affect the workings of his mind. If the thumb is short, the person vacillates from idea to idea and is indecisive. His reasoning power is poor. If the thumb is extra short, these qualities are accentuated. A short thumb with smooth fingers shows an inclination towards the fine arts, particularly, if the thumb and the fingers are conical; but if they are square or spatulate, the person may tend to be more practical, and may be inclined towards the fields of business or science or similar professions.

A normal thumb, when brought close to the palm, should extend to the middle of the third phalange of the first finger. We should also observe if it is set high or low. If set very high, it may not be long even though it may extend beyond the middle of the third phalange of the first finger.

If a thumb is long and at the same time broad, the individual may get into fits of temper (Fig. 8-A). A short and a broad thumb indicates a stubborn individual; yet the short length of the thumb also shows that 'being stubborn' is a temporary attitude and does not last long (Fig. 8-B). A slender thumb shows an artistic and refined taste. If it is flat, it endows the person with a nervous temperament and stingy nature. A very thick thumb is an indicator of lack of refinement.

Supple versus Firm-jointed Thumbs

A stiff and firm-jointed thumb (Fig. 8-C) indicates stubbornness and a lack of adaptability. Persons with such a

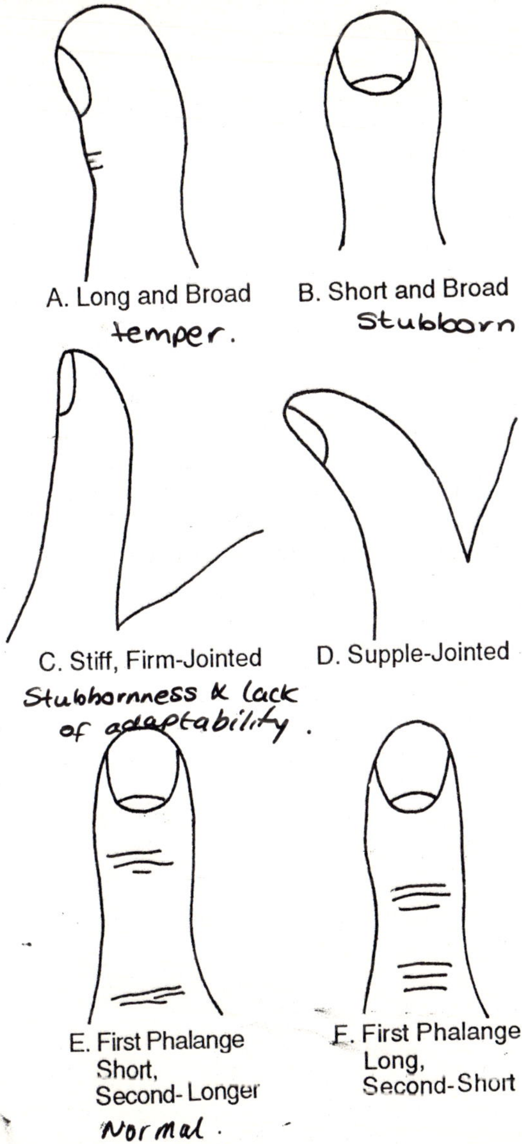
A. Long and Broad
temper.
B. Short and Broad
Stubborn.
C. Stiff, Firm-Jointed
Stubbornness & lack of adaptability.
D. Supple-Jointed
E. First Phalange Short, Second-Longer
Normal.
F. First Phalange Long, Second-Short

Fig 8

thumb are economical, persevering, determined, and faithful in love, though they may not necessarily exhibit their affections openly. Persons with a supple-jointed thumb (Fig. 8-D) are lavish, accommodating, and adapt easily with new persons and environments. They lack the perseverance and determination of people with a firm-jointed thumb.

The Phalanges

Phalanges are the narrowing bones that make up the shape of the fingers and are separated by the joints. Though the four fingers of the hand have three phalanges, the thumb has two and is, therefore, generally not referred to as a finger by anatomists.

The second phalange, measured from the rear-side of the thumb, extends from where it joins the palm (second joint) to the first joint. The first phalange is measured from the first joint to the tip of the nail. In a normal hand, the second phalange is longer than the first phalange. The proportion between the lengths of the first and second phalanges is 2:3 (Fig. 8-E). If the first phalange is longer in proportion, it should be deemed as long (Fig. 8-F). If it is shorter than the above proportion, it should be deemed as short. This rule of proportionate measurements is also applicable to the second phalange.

First Phalange: This is the nail phalange. It is always associated with will-power. The different characteristics pertaining to different types of this phalange are as follows:

Short: weak will;

Very short: very weak will and lack of proper reasoning faculty;

Long: normal will-power and reasoning faculty;

Very long: strong will-power, domineering attitude, and a very uneven and angry temper.

A thumb has different shapes at its termination (the tip of the first phalange is the termination). If it is conical, it shows an inclination towards the arts, but if it is short, it is an indication of inconsistency. Work will be left unfinished by the subject. If it is square in shape, it denotes a practical attitude. A spatulate thumb shows the ability to command, but if it is short, the subject lacks the capacity to do so because he lacks will-power. A flat phalange is indicative of a nervous temperament; a slender one of refinement, and a broad one of obstinacy. If the first phalange is thick, the individual is voluptuous but is also prone to violence. A thick-set first phalange portrays brute force and murderous tendencies.

The Second Phalange: This stands for logic and reasoning, and these powers would be in direct proportion to its length—the longer the phalange, the better the power of logic and reasoning. If this phalange is thinner in the middle, the person is diplomatic and intelligent. A flat or short phalange curtails the power of reasoning. A very slender phalange may indicate nervousness, and also affect the reasoning powers adversely.

4

The Fingers

Fingers are always on display–their size, shape, and movements reveal a great deal about the personality of an individual.

There are four fingers in the hand excluding the thumb. The first finger next to the thumb is also called the index finger. Palmists also call it the Jupiter finger because the Mount of Jupiter is situated just below it (read all about mounts in Chapter 5). The second or the middle finger is next to the first. It is called the Saturn finger. The third finger is next to the middle finger and is also called the Ring finger because the wedding ring is generally worn on it. The fourth or the little finger is the last of the four. It is also called the Mercury finger, being just above the Mount of Mercury.

Long and Short Fingers

Fingers are categorised as long, short, or normal. Normal fingers show a normal aptitude and a well-balanced nature. Long fingers endow the subject with the quality of analysing and going into details. If the fingers are very long, the subject interferes in the affairs of others and finds fault with them. If the fingers are long and thin, the subject has a tendency to deceive others. If other attributes of the hand are good, the subject may become a politician or a diplomat, and may deceive people on that plane. In business, such people deceive their customers or shareholders. If it is a low kind of hand, the subject may turn out to be a pickpocket or cheat at cards. Short fingers imply quickness in arriving at a judgement and the key word for them is 'synthesis'; while for long fingers, the key word is 'analysis' (refer also to 'knots' discussed in this chapter). Very short fingers suggest primitive instincts, selfishness, and laziness. These will be found when the length of the fingers is subnormal and the fingers are thick too.

Sometimes all the four fingers are not uniformly long or short. If the first finger is abnormally long, it shows an inclination to dominate, together with political ambition. A short first finger indicates a mind unwilling to accept responsibility. An extra long second finger shows morbidity. When it is of average good length, it bestows wisdom and sobriety; however, if it is too short–it may signify a lack of balance, and the subject may have a tendency towards frivolity. A fairly proportionate third finger shows an inclination towards appreciation of beauty in the arts, but if it is too long, it indicates a disposition towards gambling and speculation. A moderately long fourth finger connotes versatility, accompanied by a command over spoken and written expression. A very short fourth finger typifies hasty judgement.

All fingers represent the qualities of their respective mounts which are under them, and their traits should be judged accordingly. Normalcy in all fingers is good. A slight excess in length is also good. But an abnormal length indicates domination of the mount. For example, an excess of self-respect may manifest itself as arrogance; caution may take the form of distrust and morbidity; cleverness may become cunningness. However it is only when one of the fingers is much longer or shorter in proportion to the others that the above principles should be applied.

Position of the Fingers

In an ideal position each finger begins above a mount. As hands are constituted, the Mount of Mercury is slightly lower in comparison with other mounts (Fig. 13). If the base of any finger is slightly lower than what it should be, the influence of the finger diminishes, and it becomes deficient in bestowing its good qualities on the subject. Conversely, when a finger starts higher up from the mount than normal, the qualities bestowed by the finger and the mount are correspondingly enhanced.

The Shapes of the Fingers

When a finger is not erect at its base, but *inclines* slightly towards its neighbouring finger, it partakes in some measure, the qualities of the finger towards which it is inclined (Fig. 9-A).

A finger *bent* laterally (from side to side) is generally so bent as to be totally inclined to its neighbouring one (Fig. 9-B). Such a finger sharpens the influence of the finger itself.

When a finger is twisted, that is, inwardly bent or bent at more than one place, it is called *crooked* (Fig. 9-C). If the finger is crooked, the good qualities of the finger are lost. A crooked first finger shows lack of respect; a crooked second finger shows an inclination to murder or morbidity bordering on hysteria; a crooked third finger misuses art for non-artistic purposes, or does not bespeak a proper appreciation of the principles of art.

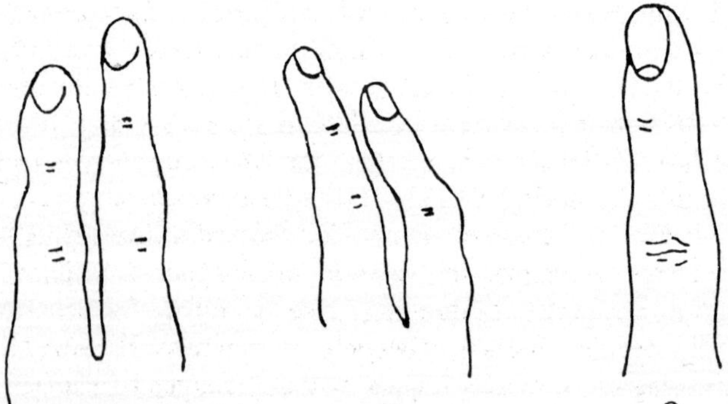

Fig 9

A crooked fourth finger is a sign of a dishonest person.

The two junction-points between two adjacent phalanges in a finger are called knots. In some hands both these junctions are knotty (Fig. 9-D). In other hands the upper junction (between the nail phalange and the middle phalange) is knotty, and the lower junction (between the middle phalange and the lower phalange) is smooth (Fig. 9-E), while in still others, both the junctions are devoid of knots, and the fingers appear smooth (Fig. 9-F). The knots in fingers are visible on the rearside of the fingers only. Fingers with knots are called *knotty fingers.*

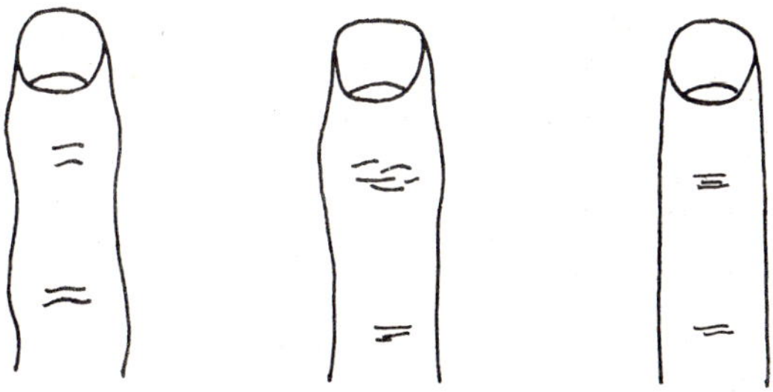

D E F

Fig 9

Persons with knotty fingers deliberate, analyse, and delve thoroughly into the pros and cons of every matter. Knots are like a sieve through which thoughts filter; the more knotty the fingers, the more will be the qualities of analysis and deliberation. This tendency is further enhanced if the fingers are long. If the fingers are smooth, there are no hurdles (knots) in the passage of thought. The subject thinks rapidly and arrives at a quick judgement. This is particularly so if the fingers are short as well. People with knotty fingers are more guided by the head and reason, while those with smooth fingers are guided by the heart and emotions.

The knot at the lower junction is called the knot of mental order, while the knot at the upper junction is referred to as that of material order. If the lower joint has a knot, it denotes a systematic and intelligent analysis of ideas, schemes, and propositions. If the upper junction has a knot, then the indication is that the subject will be systematic in household and business affairs, meticulous in dress, and methodical in daily life.

Puffy third phalanges of fingers show an appetite for eating and drinking (in communities where drinking is usual). If the third phalanges are thin or waist-shaped, the subject is finicky about his food habits.

Space between the Fingers

There may be space between the third phalanges of the fingers at the roots, when the fingers are held close to each other. If there is space between the fingers, when the fingers are close to each other, it means that the subject is liberal in spending. If the space is so wide as to allow much light to pass through the narrow chinks in-between the fingers, it means that the individual is too extravagant and will be able to save little. When the fingers are close to each other and there is no space between the fingers, this indicates miserliness.

All the above attributes are applicable when the fingers are held together. But when the subject is asked to spread out his hand naturally, the fingers will be wide apart, yet the space between no two fingers will be identical. It is, therefore, essential that, to observe the space between the fingers, the subject should be asked to spread out his hand in a natural way and not stretch out his fingers with any special effort.

When the space between the thumb and the side of the hand is rather wide, it shows independence and generosity.

Wide space between the first and second fingers also shows independence of thought.

When the space between the second and the third fingers is very wide, it indicates freedom in living, with a carefree attitude about the future. The subject is informal and not stiff.

If the space between the third and the fourth fingers is pronounced, the subject shows independence of action.

The Phalanges of the Fingers

General Features: Each finger, excluding the thumb (which has been discussed in Chapter 3), has three phalanges. Normally, the proportion between the length of the first (nail phalange), the second and the third phalange should be in the proportion of 20:35:45 (Fig. 10). If any phalange is longer than this proportion, it should be treated as long; if it is shorter than the proportion given above, it should be treated as short.

The first phalange of the fingers represents the mental outlook or the intellectual bent of mind. The second relates to the practical or business side of life, and the third to the grosser or baser qualities pertaining to the finger or the mount over which the finger is located. If the first phalange is long, the person will be devoted to mental pursuits, but if it is short, he will not be inclined towards intellectual occupations. When the second phalange is long, the business side or practical wisdom will be sharper. An excessive development of the third phalange shows the baser side of human nature, the urge for sensual pleasures and their gratification being predominant.

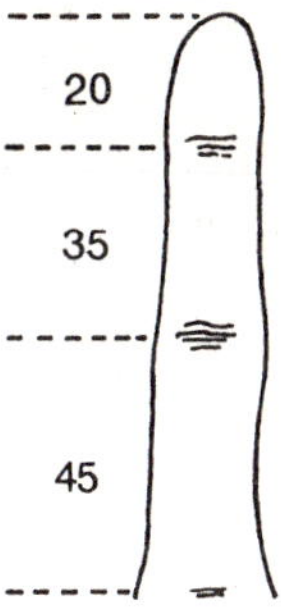

Fig 10

Individual Fingers and Their Phalanges: The phalanges of individual fingers represent different aspects. Numbers (i), (ii), and (iii) as given below, refer to the first, second, and third phalanges respectively:

Jupiter or the first finger: i) intuition and religiousness, ii) ambition and self-respect, iii) desire to dominate.

Saturn or the second finger: i) sobriety, ii) keenness in agriculture, pastoral life or a similar occupation, iii) frugality.

Sun or the third finger: i) artistic inclinations, ii) talent, iii) ostentation.

Mercury or the fourth finger: i) eloquence or flow in writing, ii) inclination towards science, iii) good aptitude for business.

If the length of the phalange is slightly above normal, there will be no negative repercussions, but an abnormal length may have the effect of taking a good quality to an extreme, and thus, negate its virtues. An excess of religious bias may make one superstitious. Self-respect may turn into vanity, and the desire to rule may take the form of dictatorship.

Over-emphasis on sobriety may turn into melancholia, and frugality may turn into miserliness. Business talent over-reaching the mark may turn to lying. Thus the abnormal length of a phalange should be interpreted in combination with other features of the hand. In case the length of a phalange is less than normal, the qualities associated with the phalange will be greatly reduced in value.

Fingertips

Fingertips can be pointed, semi-pointed or conical, square, or spatulate. When fingers are very pointed, they are called *pointed;* but when they are semi-pointed, they are called *conical.* A fingertip having a square nail with the tip being as broad as it is below it, is called a *square finger;* while one which spreads out at the tip like a spatula, is called a *spatulate finger.*

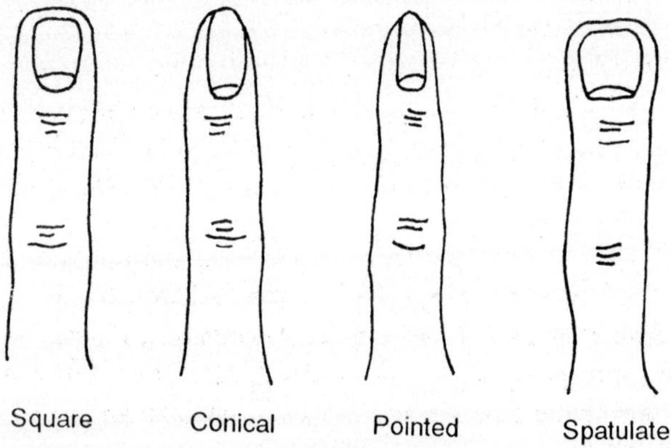

Fig 11

If the characteristics of the fingers conform to the type of hand they belong to, they are the same as have been described for the particular type of hand. But many a time it is observed that the four fingers in a hand are of different types. It is, therefore, useful to describe the traits of different types of fingertips as well.

Numbers (i), (ii), (iii), and (iv) refer to the first, second, third, and fourth fingers respectively.

Pointed: i) religious and endowed with intuitional powers, ii) melancholia and superstition, iii) an appreciation for art iv) love for science.

Conical or semi-pointed: i) love for literature, ii) religious but normal outlook on matters, iii) a keen eye for art, iv) diplomacy.

Square: i) righteousness, ii) a cautious attitude, iii) appreciation of true art, iv) potential to become a good teacher.

Spatulate: i) fond of adventure, ii) active and alert, iii) love for drama, iv) well versed in business administration.

Nails—Shapes and Characteristics

If the attributes of nails conform to the type of hands described in Chapter 2, they reflect the qualities described for the respective hands. But nails often have some additional characteristics too. These apply to all the five nails including that of the thumb.

Nails are of various shapes—square, oblong, broad, spatulate (of the shape of spatula), and so on.

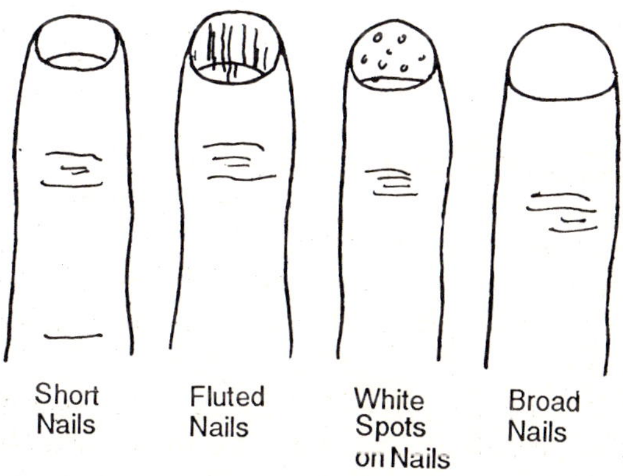

Fig 12

Short and heavy nails indicate that the subject is highly critical of others.

Fluted nails have vertical lines and allude to a nervous disorder.

White spots on the nails point to nervous disorders and loss of vitality. Big flecks of white colour on a part of the nail or on the entire nail have the same effects.

Broad nails typify muscular strength and a sound constitution.

Narrow nails belie psychic tendencies and indicate a delicate constitution.

Smaller nails which are square towards the tip and tapering towards the lower side show heart trouble.

Bluish nails with a particularly bluish colour at the base, show a weak heart. This is confirmed by a crescent-shaped mark of the moon on the nail or nails.

Pink nails represent good health and money.

Bulbous nails are those where the tip of the finger under the nail thickens and becomes hard and round. This indicates suffering from phthisis[1] or consumption.

Brittle nails signify a lack of steadiness. The subject may suffer from a nervous disorder or liver trouble. In sickness of various other types also, the nails may become brittle.

Ridges on nails have the same effect as described for fluted nails. On an average, it takes six months for the part of the nail at the root to grow up to the tip. If considered breadth-wise, half the nail will take about three months to grow out. If the ridges are on the upper half portion (towards the tip) and the lower half is healthy, it means that the ailment signified by the ridges was present three months ago. On the other hand if the lower half has ridges, it means that the ailment will continue for at least six months.

Nails growing away from the flesh are also an indication of bad health. When there is a gap between the nail and the flesh below it, it is described as growing away from the flesh. If the

1. A disease causing emaciation of the body.

gap is pronounced, it may show that the individual has a tendency to be a victim of paralysis.

Curved nails are those where the surface of the nail is slightly convex, when examined on the side of the back of the hand. They indicate throat trouble, or trouble in the bronchial region.

Reddish nails may symbolize strength and vigour; but too much reddishness of the nails and palm, along with the third phalange of the finger being thick and puffy, show a tendency towards high blood pressure.

5

The Mounts of the Hand

In a larger sense, the palm consists of the palm and fingers, including the thumb. However, the 'palm proper' is divided into the mounts and the hollow of the palm (which is described in the following chapter).

The mounts are elevated pads on the palm that appear beneath the fingers, below the thumb, and running down the side of the palm under the little finger. The puffiness, firmness, or flatness of these mounts reveal a great deal about the subject.

There are eight mounts on the palm: the Mounts of Jupiter, Saturn, Apollo (the Sun), Mercury, Upper Mount of Mars, Lower Mount of Mars, and the Mounts of Luna (the Moon) and Venus.

The mounts are named after the planets and gods and goddesses of Graeco-Roman mythology. Many astrologers and palmists believe that the mounts are influenced by these planets.

Significance of the Mounts

The level of elevation of a mount provides a key to discover the qualities of a person. A normally developed mount is good. A slightly more developed mount enhances the good qualities, but an excessively developed one may have the effect of turning

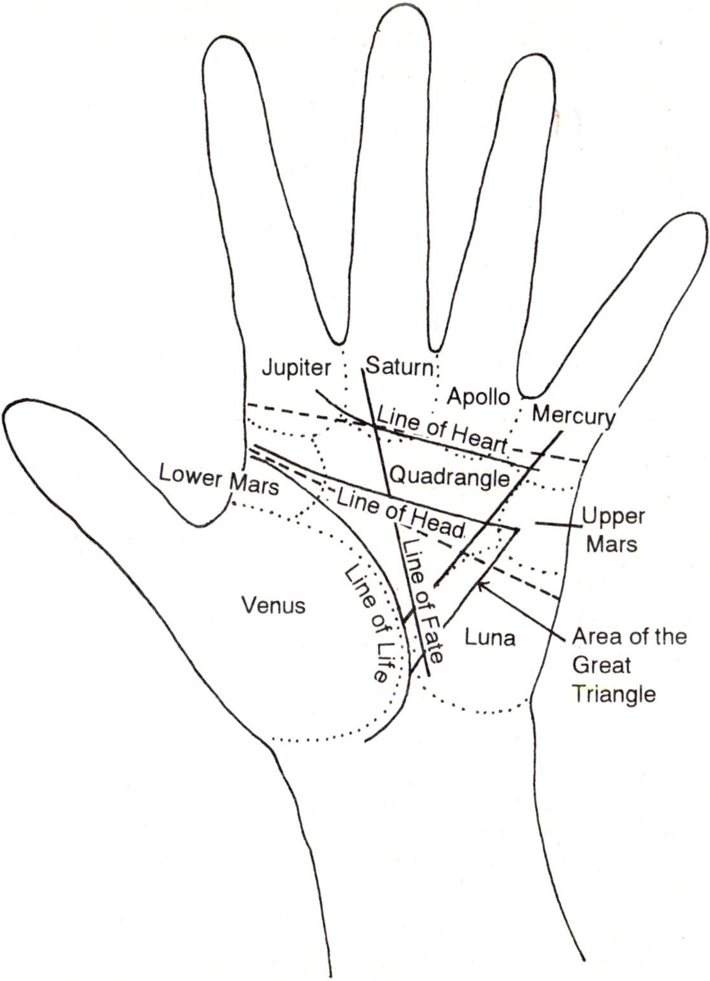

Fig 13 The Mounts of the Hand

positive qualities into negative ones. Self-respect may turn into vanity and pride, generosity into uncontrolled extravagance, hospitality into ostentatious display; prudence and caution may develop into suspicion and morbidity, and precaution into fear.

On the other hand, if a mount is inadequately developed, the good qualities will be reduced proportionately. If the mount is very depressed, the qualities pertaining to it will be present in minimal measure. We should, however, not infer that if a mount is very depressed the qualities will be altogether absent, because certain qualities are contributed not by the mounts alone, but by other features of the hand as well. For example, intelligence and a quick grasping power are features of the Mount of Mercury and of a good Line of Head too. In addition, the finger above each mount also contributes the same qualities as does the mount below it.

That brings us to the interrelationship between the finger and the mount below it. A good mount, along with a good finger above it, shows the good qualities of the mount in abundance. A good finger is one of normal size or slightly longer—strong, erect, and not bent or crooked. If either the mount or the finger is deficient, and the other strong, the deficiency of one is made up by the strength of the other; but if both the mount and the finger above it are weak or have unfavourable marks, the results are not positive, depending upon the degree of deficiency and the negative nature of the mark or marks upon them.

Before discussing each mount separately, it is essential to draw attention to one peculiarity. This peculiarity is that, in some hands, the apex on the summit of the mount is not just below the finger but slightly on one side of it. Thus the apex of the Mount of Saturn may be inclined either towards the Mount of Jupiter or the Mount of Apollo; the apex of the Mount of Apollo may be inclined towards the Mount of Saturn or Mercury; the apex of the Mount of Mercury may be towards the Mount of Apollo. The displacement of the mount from its correct position should be interpreted as follows: if the apex of the Mount of Jupiter is inclined towards the Mount of Saturn, the Jupiterean qualities inherit some qualities of Saturn. For example, one of the qualities associated with the Mount of Jupiter is pride, and Saturn is associated with introspection and introversion; so when the Mount of Jupiter is inclined towards the Mount of Saturn, these qualities will merge into self-consciousness. But if the Mount of Saturn (morbidity) leans towards the Mount of Jupiter (pride), the two qualities will enjoin as morbid pride.

The Mount of Jupiter

This mount lies at the base of the first or index finger. It stands for self-confidence, honour, pride, religion, wealth, justice, a good marriage (particularly in the hands of ladies), public life, position, generosity, discipline, growth of the body during childhood and adolescence.

If the mount is well developed, all the above qualities will be found in abundant measure, provided the finger is also of normal size, and supports the inferences drawn from the mount. If the mount is not sufficiently elevated, all the good qualities of the mount will be significantly reduced.

If the mount is excessively developed, the virtues in the various spheres described above will take a negative form. For example, self-respect and pride will turn into tyranny and dictatorship. A very highly developed mount is also a warning of diseases such as gout or high blood pressure. These can be avoided in some measure by regulating the diet and avoiding alcohol.

If the mount is very depressed and covered with fine but haphazardly marked horizontal lines, the subject will be lazy and unambitious to the extent of not making any mark in life, or advancing his interests at all. He will be selfish and irreligious.

One of the special features of a well-developed Mount of Jupiter is that it indicates better growth among children. A child with a well-developed Mount of Jupiter will grow better and earlier, and also attain puberty earlier than a child with a deficient Mount of Jupiter.

The Mount of Saturn

This mount is located below the second finger. When more developed than other mounts in the hand, the subject is endowed with Saturnian qualities such as a love for philosophy and the occult sciences; thoughtfulness, sobriety, prudence, far-sightedness, caution, diligence, power of endurance, love of solitude; gain from occupations relating to the earth like agriculture, mining, oil drilling, etc. The individual is independent, determined, patient, thrifty; inclined towards mathematics and the exact sciences rather than poetry or literature; and concise in speech and writing. These qualities are exclusive to Saturn and are not found in other planets. But they vary according to the strength or weakness of the other mounts. If the Mount of Jupiter is also strong, the subject may be a spendthrift. If the Mounts of Saturn and Mercury are both strong, the subject may be a prodigious writer. If the Mounts of Saturn and Luna are both well developed, and the Line of Head is sloping towards the Mount of Luna, the subject may write poetry tinged with pathos.

On the negative side, the disagreeable traits of Saturn are mistrust, suspicion, a melancholic nature, laziness, lack of foresight, lack of caution and prudence; belief in superstitions, irreligiousness, obstinacy, disharmony, avarice; incapacity to get on harmoniously with others; wandering about aimlessly; making liaisons with women of low social order, or with women older than the subject (if the Mount of Venus is well developed), but remaining unmarried. If the Mount of Venus is weak and depressed—loss from agriculture, mining, and products of the earth; maliciousness, cruelty, crime, etc., are indicated.

If the Mount of Saturn is excessively developed, many of the good qualities will be negated; the subject may be eccentric, and sometimes, even a crank, if the Mounts of Luna and Mercury are also depressed. In fact, in such a case, the subject is likely to be morbid, discontented, too much of an introvert, and unsuccessful in the practical world. He may become a recluse and shun society.

If the mount is less developed than normal, the positive qualities will be present, though in lesser measure. If the mount is very depressed, negative traits will be in evidence. Negative traits will be even more enhanced if a bad sign such as a girdle is present.

The Mount of Apollo

The Mount of Apollo or the Sun is adjacent to the Mount of Saturn in the anti-clockwise order, and is located below the third finger. This has, from time immemorial, been associated with the sun and arts. The true solar qualities are found in abundant measure when the mount is well developed, and there is a strong third or solar finger, as well as a good Line of Apollo.

This mount stands for artistic qualities like singing, dancing, music, painting, sculpture, authorship of books; a high position in life; political advancement; and gain from high-ranking people in society.

The ancient Hindus associated this mount with education and learning. However, whether an individual will make a mark in some sphere of life or not, depends not only upon a well-developed Mount of Apollo, but also upon other accessory factors in the hand. For example, in a good musician's hand, it is not only the Mount of Apollo that is well developed; the Mounts of Luna and Venus are also prominent, and the Line of Head is inclined towards the Mount of Luna. To excel at dancing and have a strong physique, a well-elevated Mount of Mercury and a proportionate little finger are also important. A good Mount of Apollo—along with a good Line of Head, a well-developed Mount of Mercury, and a long fourth finger having a long first phalange which is rounded on the inner side—may make one a distinguished author. These examples are illustrative but not exhaustive. Ultimately it is a combination of factors that decides what course an individual's life will take.

A well-developed Mount of Apollo makes the subject sensitive, hasty, short-tempered, sincere, sympathetic, and obliging. He is dignified in speech and manners. He is liberal in religious matters. He has strong likes and dislikes. His marriage is successful.

It may by reiterated that an excessive development of this mount may lead to pride, vanity, and ostentation. An under-developed mount will lessen the effect of the good qualities described for this mount. A circle on this mount or on the Line of Heart below this mount may lead to loss of vision. From the health point of view, this mount is connected with weak vision and palpitation of the heart.

The Mount of Mercury

The Mount of Mercury is located beneath the little finger. Mercury signifies transmission of thought, quick activity of the nervous system, effective communication through speech and writing, transportation of goods and men, and movement.

As such a subject having a well-developed Mount of Mercury will be quick in his thoughts and actions. He will function well in any capacity where quick thinking is required. He may excel as a lawyer, a sportsman, a journalist, or a publisher, or even become an effective public speaker, or an accomplished author. He may achieve success in the postal or railway service, or in a profession associated with transport by road, sea or air, because one of the key words associated with Mercury is transmission. He will be fond of travelling.

People with a prominent Mount of Mercury can be successful brokers, commission agents, salesmen, authors, translators, spokesmen. They may also make good businessmen if the third phalange of the Mercury finger is normal.

Mercurians are alert and quick, and their nervous system responds to quickness; so, they do well in games and sports where nimbleness is required. But in sports where muscular strength is necessary, such as weightlifting or throwing a disc, they do not excel.

The mercurial quality in individuals with a favourable Mount of Mercury makes them fond of change. They are good at imitating others, either in speech, writing, or personal behaviour. A good Mount of Mercury also shows an ability for astrology, mathematics, accounts, statistics, and the physical sciences. Such people make good doctors and nurses.

If the Mount of Mercury is deficient and underdeveloped, all the good qualities will be minimized. Negative marks on the mount may produce evil effects. The subject may boast of only a very superficial knowledge, but may try to conceal it by being garrulous, or even a liar. He will suffer from poor mental concentration, and may be found lacking in application. As a result, he may turn dishonest.

Mercury in the Zodiac is the lord of the sixth sign, Virgo. So a defective Mount of Mercury indicates diseases of the liver and of the nervous system.

The Mount of Mars

While all other mounts have been assigned one location, the Mounts of Mars have been assigned two. The space between the Mounts of Jupiter and Venus is called the Lower Mount of Mars, and that between the Mounts of Mercury and the Luna—the Upper Mount of Mars.

The Mounts of Mars represent the bone marrow and the blood. They also represent energy, valour, daring, prowess, and fearlessness. They stand for generosity in spending and a domineering attitude. As the word 'martial' is derived from Mars, it signifies a fighting spirit. The Lower Mount of Mars endows the subject with energy, courage, and aggressive powers; while the Upper Mount instils in him consistency and perseverance in resisting the onslaughts of others. We may, in short, distinguish the Lower and Upper mounts as being offensive and defensive, respectively.

The Mounts of Mars have no finger to support or spoil their effects. But the will-power has a lot to do with the martial spirit, and for this, the examination of the upper phalange of the thumb is very necessary. If this phalange is long and strong, it will strengthen the good qualities of the mounts.

An excessive development of the Lower Mount may make one quarrelsome. This applies to the Upper one too. Moderately well-developed mounts may have all the good martial qualities as stated above. But an excessive development of the mounts shows an inclination towards violence, and tends to make one materialistic and harsh.

Mars is connected with fire, and well-developed Mounts of Mars also favour service in factories where fire is an essential component of the industry. People who have depleted Mounts of Mars are usually timid, and lacking in courage and pioneership. Since they also lack perseverance, they stop halfway on the road to success. A person with well-formed Mounts of Mars is confident, dignified, and courageous, but persons with defective mounts are rough in manners and speech, irresolute, and quarrelsome.

The Mount of Luna

The Mount of Luna or the Moon lies just below the Upper Mount of Mars and extends to the bracelets. It is opposite the Mount of Venus, on the little finger side of the palm. Like the Mount of Venus, the Mount of Luna being watery, commonly shows similar traits of harmony, poetry, attachment to females; fastidiousness in taste, dress and surroundings; appreciation of the arts; gain from aqueous products, etc. The aesthetics of Venus pertain more to the senses, while those of Luna relate to the imagination.

A well-formed Mount of Luna endows the subject with a vivid imagination. A sloping Line of Head towards the Mount of Luna makes a man a lover; but if melancholia is denoted by the Mount of Saturn and the second finger, then the subject tends towards lunacy. If intellectualism is shown by other indications of the hand, the subject could become a poet.

A fairly well-developed Mount of Luna would make one fond of travelling by water. Well-formed Mounts of Venus and Luna signify an inclination towards dress-making; trading in silk, aerated waters, drinks, liquors, white articles; gardens, flowers, etc.

A fairly-developed Mount of Luna indicates imagination, feeling, idealism, and romance; but when not in control, it may lead to an unbridled imagination, and, therefore, less physical capacity for arduous work. An excessive development is also an impediment to the study of mathematics and the exact sciences.

If the Mounts of Luna, Mercury and Saturn are afflicted, the subject may suffer from insanity or paralysis. If only the Mount of Luna is severely afflicted, the subject may become a victim of epilepsy or kidney trouble, or diseases connected with the ovaries and the bladder.

Negative markings on the Mount of Luna show an unhealthy imagination, garrulousness, and a tendency towards perversion of the truth.

The Mount of Venus

The Mount of Venus is located at the root of the thumb. It is entirely encircled by the Line of Life which is called the Lower Mount of Mars (as explained earlier). The more curved the Line of Life is, the more space it will surround, making the mount a large one. On the physical plane the Mount of Venus signifies sex and virility; on the mental plane it stands for aesthetics; and on the spiritual plane it represents love, undiluted with sensuality.

The subject's attraction to the opposite sex can be gauged from the Mount of Venus and the Line of Heart. The extent to which the aesthetic sense is developed can be measured from the Mounts of Luna and Venus, and also from the Mount and finger of Apollo in a conical hand. The spiritual tendencies of the subject are observed from the Mounts of Jupiter, Venus, and Saturn.

If elastic to the touch and well formed, the Mount of Venus denotes a good and comfortable life. It indicates amiability, sociability, and harmony. If other indications point to the subject becoming an artist, he will excel as one, because Venus is synonymous with love and beauty. If the Mount of Venus is predominant and the fingers are thick, the subject may do well in the culinary arts. Venus is connected with reproduction. In a male hand it stands for virility. Therefore, if in a man's hand, a part of the mount has sunk, it means that his virility is at a low ebb. In a woman's hand this may mean a reduction in the reproductive capacity.

However the Mount of Venus has to be examined in coordination with the shape of the hand, fingers, other mounts, and markings. A coarse Mount of Venus with a girdle may mean too much sensuousness.

Bad marks on the palm are an indication of loose morals. If the skin is coarse and the muscles flabby, the subject is lazy.

6

The Plain of Mars

The central position of the palm, which is generally depressed due to the elevation of the mounts all around, is known as the hollow of the hand or the Plain of Mars (since it connects the Upper and Lower Mounts of Mars). Western palmists have assigned positions in the hand to the seven planets; but Hindu palmists have assigned the Plain of Mars to Rahu and Ketu.

If we divide the Plain of Mars into two parts, the area between the Lines of Head and Heart is called the Quadrangle; the remaining portion of the Plain is called the Great Triangle (Fig. 13).

The Quadrangle

The quadrangular area between the Lines of Head and Heart should be smooth with few lines crossing it, wide at both ends, as well as at the centre. If the Quadrangle is wide towards the ends, it shows a straightforward disposition. If the space between the Lines of Head and Heart is too wide, it typifies a person who is independent and generous. A very narrow Quadrangle denotes meanness and miserliness.

It should be borne in mind that the Quadrangle is wide, either due to the Line of Head being too low, or due to the Line of Heart being too high. If the Line of Head is too low, the native's reasoning power will be affected adversely. The second phalange of the thumb should also be examined in this connection. If the Line of Heart is too high, the subject will be sensuous and jealous.

Similarly if the Quadrangle is very narrow due to the Line of Head being too high, the native will be narrow-minded, bigotted, and judgemental. His heart will rule his head. But if the Line of Heart is too high, the head will rule the heart and, consequently, the native will be stingy.

A very narrow Quadrangle also shows a tendency towards diseases like asthma.

The Great Triangle

The Great Triangle is formed by the Lines of Life, Head, and Health. If the Line of Health is absent, as is frequently the case, its place is filled by an imaginary line to form the base of the Triangle, otherwise the Line of Apollo forms the base (Fig. 13).

Three angles are formed in the Great Triangle by the Lines of Life, Head, and Health. The first or upper angle is formed by the Lines of Life and Head; the second or middle angle is formed by the Lines of Head and Health; the third or lower angle is formed by the Lines of Health and Life.

When the Great Triangle is well formed by the Lines of Life, Head, and Health, it denotes a good future and longevity. A good Line of Life ensures a long life; a well-developed Line of Head indicates broad-minded thinking; a sound Line of Health signifies good health. All these contribute greatly towards a good livelihood. If any of the lines is defective, the positive effects related to that line will not be realised.

7

The Lines of the Hand Characteristic Features

The lines of the hand are divided into two types: the Major Lines are the Line of Life, Line of Head, Line of Heart, and Line of Fate; the Minor Lines include the Lines of Marriage, Children, Sun, Health, etc. There are a variety of beginnings and endings to these lines, as well as markings, defects, and characteristics—all of which tell us something different about a person. There are also some general characteristics which are common to all lines.

The location of a mark or defect on a line provides an idea of the approximate age at which the impact of that mark or defect will be felt.

When the mark is at the commencement of a line, the effect is felt in the early part of life; if the mark is at the middle or at the end of a line, then the effect is felt during the middle or end of life, respectively. The method of ascertaining of age, as indicated by the various lines, is discussed in subsequent chapters.

Absence of Lines

The three major lines—the Lines of Life, Head, and Heart—are always found in hands. When we say 'always', we mean almost always, for in a few hands we have examined, the Line of Heart was absent. In such peculiar hands there was only one line in place of the Lines of Head and Heart. The line was in the place where the Line of Head is usually located. On such a hand the interpretation would be that the Lines of the Head and Heart had merged.

A missing Line of Heart indicates that the subject is lacking in sympathy and affection for others.

The Line of Head is always found in all hands, though in some cases, it may be very short. We have not come across any case where the Line of Life was absent. If it is absent, however, it means that the subject lives on nervous energy.

Besides these three major lines, other lines may or may not be present in the hand. The absence of a Line of Fate does not mean that there will be no wealth, but wealth in such cases will be earned by hard labour. The absence of the Line of Liver or the Line of Health is an indication of good health. The Via Lascivia, the Line of Intuition, the Girdle of Venus, and the Ring of Solomon or Saturn are found in very few hands. The Line of Union is generally present.

Types of Lines

Branches: When a line splits into two or three parts which are almost as thick as the main line, and the split lines proceed at a distance from each other, they are called *branches* of the main line. Branches may be short or long. Those proceeding towards the mounts are called *ascending branches* (Fig. 14), while those moving in the lower direction towards the wrist are called *descending branches* (Fig. 14).

Off-Shoots: Fine and thin lines which branch off from the main line are called *off-shoots* (Fig. 14).

Both branches and off-shoots denote a change—a new course in life. If a branch or off-shoot proceeds towards and reaches a mount, it means that the person at the age indicated by the branch or off-shoot, will have a great fascination for the person or the subject represented by the mount.

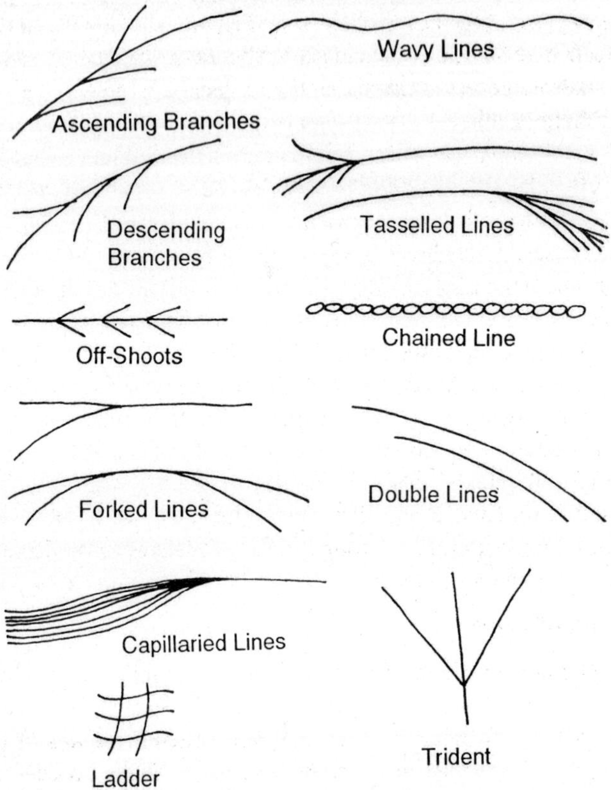

Fig 14 Type of Lines

Fork: When a line splits into two branches at the beginning or at the end, it is called a *fork* (Fig. 14). When the two prongs are small, it is called a fork, but when the two prongs are long, they are called branches. A fork is generally found at the end of a line (Fig. 15-MM), and, sometimes, at the commencement

---

1. The end of a horizontal line is towards the side of the little finger; the commencement of a horizontal line is towards the thumb side. The end of a vertical line is towards the fingers; while the commencement is towards the bracelets.

(Fig. 15-HH). It is also a favourable feature for the Line of Heart to have a fork at its commencement (Fig. 15-HH). A Line of Fate which has a fork at its commencement (Fig. 15-FF) would indicate some person assisting the subject in his fortune; a fork at the end would signify fortune from two sources, indicated by the mounts towards which the forks go. If the forks split into two before reaching the mounts, it simply means diversion into two channels.

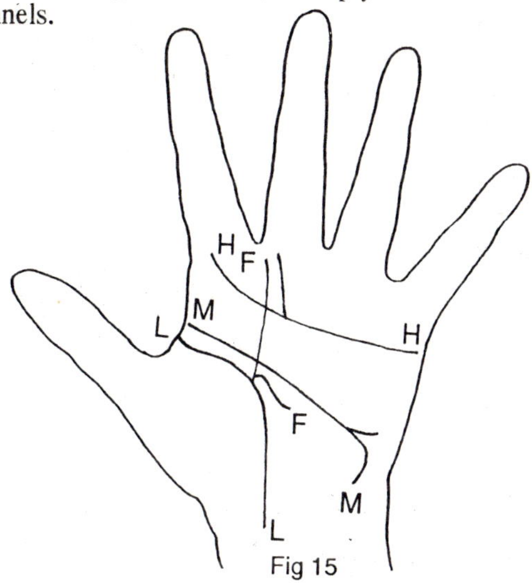

Fig 15

Capillaried Lines: Very thin, hair-like lines are called *capillaried lines.* When one of the main lines has continuous, thin, hair-like off-shoots throughout its length, it is called a capillaried line (Fig. 14). Capillaried lines weaken the main line if the capillaries go towards the direction of the wrist.

Ladder: Two small parallel lines cut across by two or three small lines, giving the appearance of a ladder, are called *laddered lines* (Fig. 14).

A Broken Line: A *break* in a line is a serious defect, indicating adverse circumstances in relation to matters which the line signifies (Fig. 16 A). The adverse circumstances last during the period indicated by the position of the break.

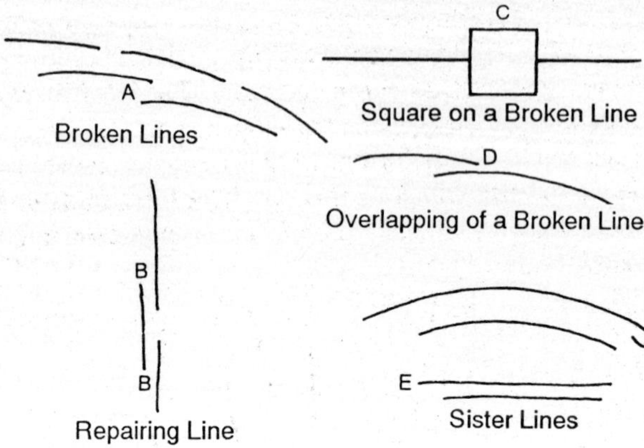

Fig 16 Breaks in Lines

There are only four ways in which the harm caused by a break can be mitigated.

1. When another short line runs parallel to the main line at a short distance from it and covers the break (Fig.16-BB), the defect of the break is repaired. The short line is known as the **repairing line.** The effect of the repairing line may be explained as follows: suppose the roof of a room is broken, but there is another roof above that to cover the broken roof, then the rain water will not fall into the room. A *repairing line* works in a similar manner.

2. The mark of a **square** also removes the harmful effect of a *break*. If there is a square made by four small lines enclosing the break (Fig. 16-C), the defect caused by the break is removed.

3. When the two broken ends of the line **overlap** each other (Fig. 16-D), then too, the defect caused by the break is deemed to be repaired. Some kind of change in the affairs governed by the line would take place, though the overlapping would ensure that no serious consequences would follow.

4. When there is a break in the line, and the broken end turns towards its source, making a hook-like appearance, it is a very serious defect indicating serious damages. This defect is repaired by a sister line to the main line or a square.

A Sister Line: A long line running parallel to the main line, though not of the same length, is called a *sister line* (Fig. 16-E). For example, the Line of Mars is a sister line to the Line of Life. Many palmists even call the Line of Apollo a sister line of the Line of Fate.

Trident: A line which splits into three prongs at the end is called a trident. An independent mark resembling a trident, formed by short, thin lines, and found anywhere on the palm, is also called a trident (Fig. 14).

A Wavy or Zig-zag Line: An undulating line consisting of, or showing an alternate or contrary curve is called *wavy or zig-zag*. It is neither straight nor curved, but takes abrupt alternate right and left turns (Fig. 14).

An Even Line: A good line of uniform width and depth and without any flaws is called an *even line*. Such a line shows vigour and steadfastness. The subject is purposeful and attains success, particularly, when the line is well coloured.

A Thin Line: A line is called *thin* when it is very finely marked. The Lines of Life, Head, and Heart are more deeply marked than, for example, the Line of Influence. So even though a thin Line of Life, Head, or Heart may appear to be thicker than a Line of Influence, it will still be called *thin*. In other words, when a line is thinner than its normal width or thickness, it is called thin.

Broad and Shallow Lines: Lines may be deep or shallow. Shorter lines, such as the Line of Influence, are thin. But the Lines of Life, Head, and Heart, being long lines, could be broad and shallow.

Broad and shallow lines show weakness and lack of vigour. Persons with such lines do not pursue their objectives with steadfastness or sufficient energy, thereby often meeting with failure. This is particularly so when the lines are poorly coloured.

If a line is broad and shallow at its commencement, but becomes *even* at a later stage, the effects relating to an *Even Line* are experienced during the ages corresponding to the two different qualities of the line.

When the same line is deep for part of its course, and not so deeply cut at another place in its course, it is called an **uneven line.** It will exert a good influence upto the stage where it is deeply cut, but the good effects will decrease proportionately as the line becomes shallower.

When a line splits, and the splinter, whether short or long, reduces the evenness of the parent line from which the splinter emanates, the influence of the main line is weakened. But if the splinter is vertical and proceeds upwards, it does not reduce the evenness or the good character of the main line. It reduces the effect of the good qualities of the main line if it moves downwards.

Tassel: If a line ends in a number of small lines, it is called a *tassel.* A tassel symbolizes dissipation or diffusion of energy. It also signifies that the qualities associated with the line in question have become very weak (Fig. 14). If the tassel is encased in a square, it means protection from the harmful effects of the tassel.

A Chained Line: If a line appears to be formed by the joining together of several links, the portion that is linked together is called a *chained line* (Fig. 14). It is not necessary that a line be chained throughout its course.

If the Line of Life is chained, it denotes a susceptibility to illness or continued ill health. A chained Line of Head points to vacillation and lack of a firm determination. If the Line of Heart is chained, it illustrates a flirtatious nature, and indicates disappointments in love. A chained Line of Fate does not bode well for success in the subject's career and capability to earn money.

A Double Line: If, instead of there being one line, there are two almost parallel lines running in the same course, they are called *double lines* (Fig. 14). Some people have double Lines of Fate or double Lines of Head.

Double lines should not be confused with *Sister Lines.* The distinctive factor is that the sister lines are not so prominent. When there are two equally prominent parallel lines, and it is difficult to distinguish which is the principal line and which is the auxiliary—they are called *double lines.*

Marks on Lines and Mounts

There may be certain marks found on lines or mounts, or on the Plain of Mars, or on the inner side of the fingers and the thumb. These marks may resemble the shape of a cross, a grille, a dot, an island, a triangle, a spot, a circle, or a square.

An Island: Any two curved lines enclosing a space form an *island.* An island is formed when, at a certain stage, a line splits into two, and after proceeding for some length, joins again to form a single line. The area covered by the split sections of the line, enclosing some space, and forming a small enclosure, is called an *island* (Fig. 17-A). Sometimes an island is also formed by two unrelated lines crossing each other (Fig. 17-B).

An island indicates an impediment in matters signified by the line or mount on which it is formed. For example, if it is on the Line of Fate, it would cause a fall in income during that period; if it is on the Line of Life, it would imply a set-back in health; if on the Line of Head, it would be an indication of mental trouble, and so on.

Triangle: The mark of a *triangle* is the same as in geometry (Fig. 17). A triangle is considered to be a good mark; it adds to the good qualities of the line, mount, or finger where it is found. For example, if it is on the Mount of Jupiter, it will enhance the good qualities of the mount; if found on the Line of Fate, it increases wealth; and if it is located on the little finger, the Mercurian qualities are increased. A triangle enhances the mental qualities, and if it is found on the Line of Life, it should be interpreted as mental brilliance.

Cross-bars: Several short lines running in close proximity and parallel to each other horizontally constitute a *cross-bar* (Fig. 17). A cross-bar is a serious defect because its harmful effect is unmitigated by any other sign or line.

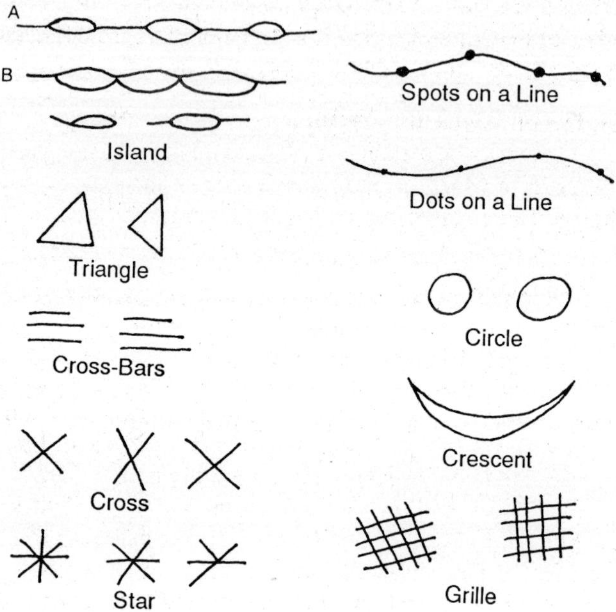

Fig 17 Marks on Lines and Mounts

Cross: It is a defect, and if it is on the Line of Life or on the Line of Health, it may signify a danger to health (Fig. 17). Some special effects of a *cross* are discussed in the chapter on Mounts.

Star: If two or three prongs more are added to a cross, and all the prongs meet at the centre, they constitute a *star* (Fig. 17). A big star is not considered auspicious. Even a small star should be well formed to produce good effects. Special positive influences of stars have been discussed in subsequent chapters.

Spot: A discoloured *spot*—whether big or small—shows trouble with the purity of the blood. If it is found on a line (Fig. 17), it means that the good qualities of the line are negated at the age indicated by the spot. Special indications on mounts are discussed in subsequent chapters.

Dot: A *dot* is of the size of the point of a pencil or bigger, on a line or anywhere in the palm. A dot indicates a defect on the line on which it is found. Very small dots on the Lines of Life, Head, or Heart mean illness at the age indicated by the dot. The dots may be just pinpoint depressions, or may be coloured. If a dot is formed on a mount, it spoils the good qualities of the mount.

There is a change in interpretation according to the colour of the dot. Deep red or blue dots denote illness (Fig. 17). Yellow dots indicate nervous tension. White ones are not so bad.

Trident: As explained earlier, a line, whether major or minor, which splits into three short lines at the end is called a *trident* (Fig. 14). A trident is good when found on the upper end of a line. For example, if the Line of Fate or the Line of Apollo ends in a trident, it adds to the brilliancy of the lines.

Circle: The sign of a *circle* is rare (Fig. 17). But if it is present on the Line of Life or the Mount of Apollo, it indicates loss of eyesight. All blind persons do not have it, but the circle is a sign of loss of vision.

Crescents: The *crescent* in the form of a new moon (Fig. 17) symbolises inconsistency and removals. If it is found on the ring finger, it denotes a literary vocation; if it is on the Line of Apollo, it signifies a leaning towards music. Crescents, if joined with the upper side of the Line of Heart, are an indication of a boil or a wound on the back.

Grille: Three, four, or more thread-like thin lines cut across by another two, three, four lines, and producing a mesh-like appearance anywhere on the palm or fingers, constitute a *grille* (Fig. 17). The lines making a grille—both vertical and horizontal—are very thin and small.

A grille is a very serious defect. If it is on a mount, the good qualities signified by the mount are greatly diminished, and the bad traits are largely enhanced. For example, a good Mount of Jupiter infuses self-confidence and a generous temperament, but the presence of a grille will negate these qualities, and the native will be arrogant, conceited, and ostentatious. Or the person may have health defects pertaining to the mount. For example, if it is on the Mount of Jupiter, it may cause ill health due to gluttony and luxurious living. While estimating the degree of effect of a grille, it is necessary to study the constituent vertical and horizontal parts. If the vertical lines cut across the horizontal lines, it is not so harmful as when horizontal lines cut the vertical lines. Only a minute examination of the lines will reveal this aspect.

Single Line: A single vertical line uncrossed on a mount increases its good qualities.

The general characteristics of marks have been discussed in this chapter. If, on a mount, a mark indicates something different to the effects stated above, these are discussed in Chapter 17.

8

Major Lines of the Hand
The Line of Life

The Line of Life is one of the most important and prominent of lines, along with the Lines of Head, Heart and Fate. It starts generally from the mid-point of the roots of the thumb and the index finger, traverses in the form of a sector of a circle and ends at the base of the palm near the bracelet (Fig. 18). This is the usual course, but the actual course and whether it covers within it, a wide area of the palm or a narrower one, differs from hand to hand. The Line of Life, as the name shows, indicates the life force.

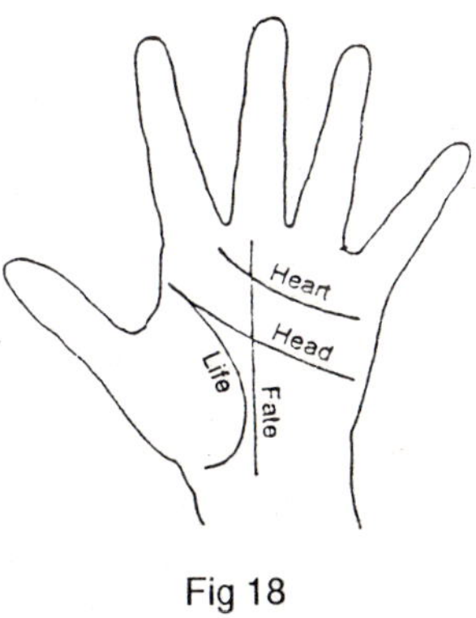

Fig 18

Characteristics

The Line of Life should be long, narrow, and deep. The opposite of a deep and well-cut line is a line which is broad and shallow. It should also be borne in mind that if the hand is soft, it indicates less resistance to illness. A flabby hand shows laziness, and an elastic hand, energy. People with a broad and

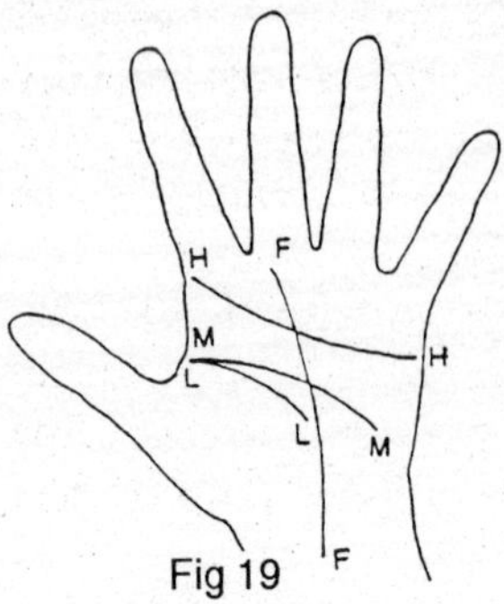

Fig 19

shallow Line of Life (Fig. 19) do not have robust health and vitality, and, consequently, lack in self-confidence and energy which are so necessary in life for success and achievement.

The colour of the Line of Life indicates certain propensities which are given below:

Pink: good health;
Red: febrile diseases[1];
Blue: poor circulation of blood, heart disease;
Yellow: liver trouble, irritability;

It should be remembered that, for wealth, not only the mounts and the Line of Fate, but also the Line of Life have to be examined. Success in ninety-nine per cent cases is symbolised by energy, perseverance, and assiduous application, but when the Line of Life is broad and shallow (Fig. 20-LL), the subject is not physically strong enough to have the above qualities in sufficient measure. When the life force is weak, the subject also lacks mental strength.

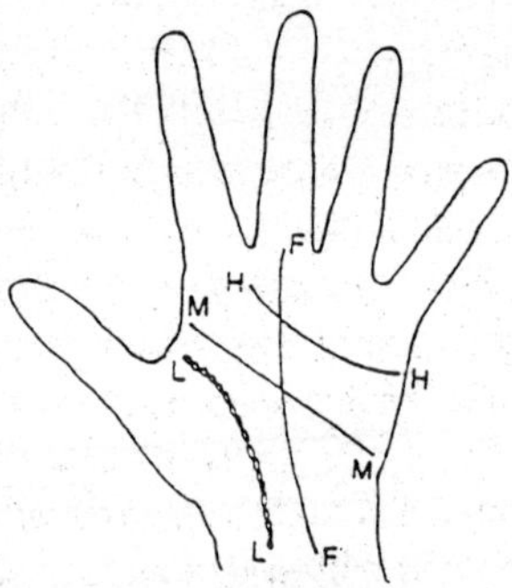

Fig 20

Though a deep and clear-cut Line of Life shows good health, physical strength and vigour, if the Mount of Venus is also very highly developed, then the subject may waste himself in excessive sexual indulgence. A strong Line of Life provides better powers of digestion, but if the third phalange of the fingers is thick and long, then the native's habit of taking rich

1. Relating to fever.

foods may make him suffer from blood pressure. If only the third phalange of the Jupiter finger is strong and the palm is very pink, then the subject, due to his being too fond of food and drinks, may suffer from apoplexy. This is also the case when the Upper Mount of Mars is overdeveloped.

A narrow and thin Line of Life also shows that the life force is subnormal. A subject with such a narrow and thin line cannot put up with much physical hardship as he lacks endurance. The weak life force makes him susceptible to illness. Due to lack of normal energy, he is also lazy.

When the Line of Life appears to be made up of several fine lines (Fig. 21-LL) instead of one deep and well-cut line, it is also a sign of weakness in the life force and, therefore, of general debility, delicacy of health, and a nervous temperament. What is nervousness? When the nerves are weak or easily agitated due to their lacking steadiness, the subject is said to have a nervous disposition. A healthy body has healthy nerves. The case is reversed when health suffers.

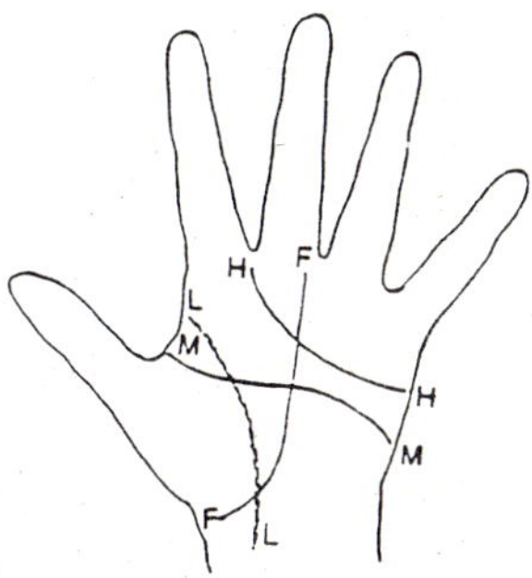

Fig 21

A chained Line of Life (Fig. 22-LL) is also considered defective. There are likely to be physical ailments during the period that the line is chained. People who have suffered from illness during childhood have a Line of Life which is chained or defective at the commencement. If the Line of Life is chained upto a certain distance, and the rest of it is smooth and free from defects, then ill health can be accurately predicted upto the stage where it is chained. During those years, the subject might have

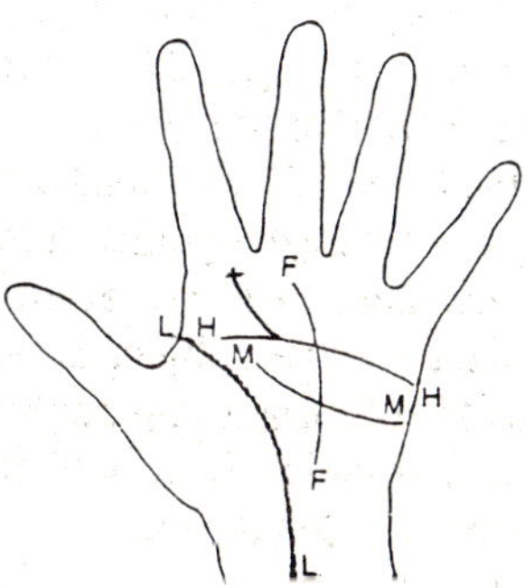

Fig 22

been continuously ill, but may have had delicate health, suffering from illnesses only now and then. If the line is not only chained but also broad and shallow, then it is still worse; for in such a case, two impairing factors are combined. The indications with regard to a chained Line of Life should be applied to a ladder-like Line of Life also.

Course of the Line

Commencement: Generally the Line of Life commences at the side of the hand under the Mount of Jupiter, encircles the Lower Mount of Mars and Venus, and ends at the base of the hand; but when, instead of commencing from there, it starts from the Mount of Jupiter (Fig. 23-LL), it indicates pride and ambition.

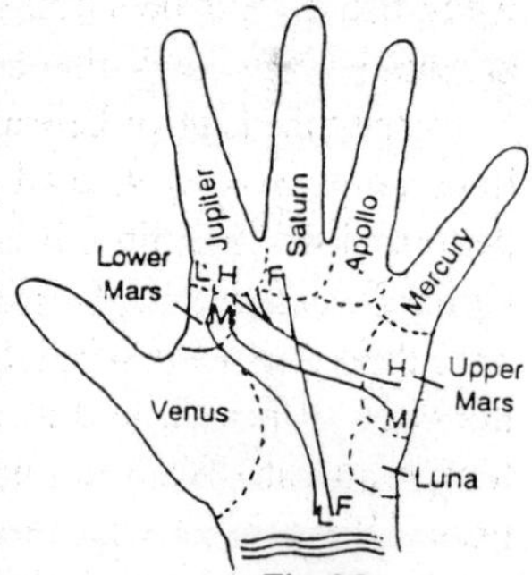

Fig 23

When the Line of Life is joined with the Line of Head at the commencement (Fig. 24-LL, MM), it shows that the subject is fairly intelligent and exercises logic and reason in his decisions. He is, however, also very sensitive. It also shows his lack of independence. When there is a very wide gap between the commencing points of the Lines of Life and Head, the native is over-independent to the point of rashness, and refuses to heed the advice of others.

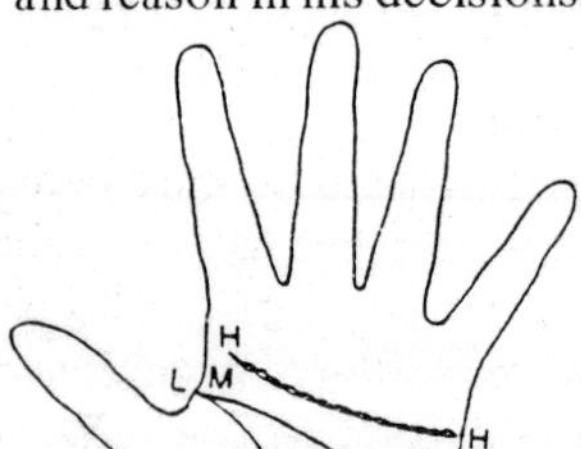

Fig 24

If the Lines of Life, Head, and Heart are all joined together at the commencement, it is not at all a good sign, for the subject is not cautious and prudent, but so hasty that he often gets into trouble, and his decisions are, at times, catastrophic. Such a three-pronged commencement also indicates sudden death.

Curvature: The course of the Line of Life is circular. The bigger the circle, the more the space it encloses on the Mount of

Venus (Fig. 25-LL). In other words, the Mount of Venus will be larger and, hence, the vigour, virility, fondness for the opposite sex, aesthetic sense, warmth or affection, and other qualities of Venus will be found in abundant measure in the personality of the subject. But if the Line of Life has a small curvature, and goes rather straight to the base of the hand (Fig. 24-LL), it encloses a small space and, consequently, the Mount of Venus will be small. Such a line indicates meagreness in all matters pertaining to vigour, vitality, fondness for the opposite sex, etc., which have been enumerated above.

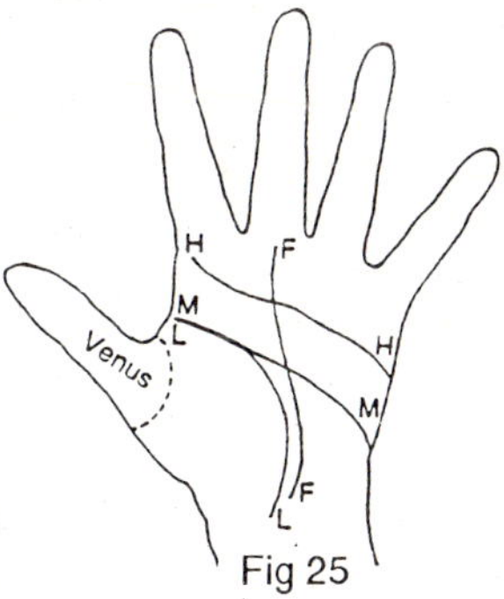

Fig 25

Three principles must be remembered in this connection. A large Mount of Venus has the contrary effect. So if the curvature of the Line of Life is big, resulting in greater space enclosed by it, it is an indication that the subject will have a large number of children. But if the Line of Life is almost straight, making the Mount of Venus narrow, it means that fertility is low, even resulting in sterility in many female hands.

The other point which merits attention is that Venus stands for affluence, wealth, a comfortable life, luxurious paraphernalia, and worldly pleasures. So a long Line of Life enclosing a wider space on the Mount of Venus, predicts a comfortable life materially, while a comparatively straight line enclosing a small space on the Mount of Venus shows the reverse, namely, want of comforts and pleasures in life.

The third principle is that, the longer the Line of Life and the more well marked it is, the longer will be the lifespan. But if the Line of Life is short, particularly in both the hands, longevity is likely to be cut short. Here again it may be observed that many persons who had a long Line of Life have died a premature death.

The explanation for this can be found in the palm itself. Death is caused either by a gradual ebb of vital energy, or by sudden causes such as heart trouble or an accident. When death is due to gradual decay and deterioration, the Line of Life will fully indicate it; but where it is due to sudden causes such as heart failure (though the man may seem to be in robust health), it will be indicated in the Line of Heart. Thus there are many such instances such as serious illnesses that cause sudden death, which may not be indicated in the Line of Life.

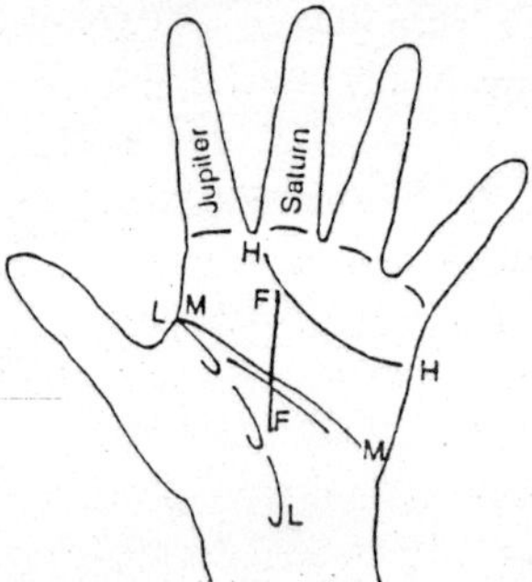

Fig 26

Termination: When the Line of Life runs its course for some distance, and then turns back for a short distance, making a kind of a hook (Fig. 26-LL) at the lower end where it turns back, then also, it signifies a great set-back to physical vigour and vitality, and may even indicate death if other indications on the hand conform to similar indications.

A Line of Life which becomes gradually faint towards the end is a sign of loss of vigour and vitality at the corresponding age that the line becomes faint. If the line ends in a tassel (Fig. 27-LL), then also, it shows a diffusion and weakening of the life force and scattered energy, resulting in general debility and loss of vitality.

When the Line of Life appears to be deep, clear-cut, and strong till the end, and when there is no indication available with regard to the termination of life, the Lines of Head and Heart should be checked for marks such as those of an island, a cross, a deep cut, or a dot on them, and the time of death can then be predicted accurately. However, we should not waste our time in trying to locate such marks because in so many hands that we examined, the Line of Life continued to be deep, strong, and well cut throughout; but

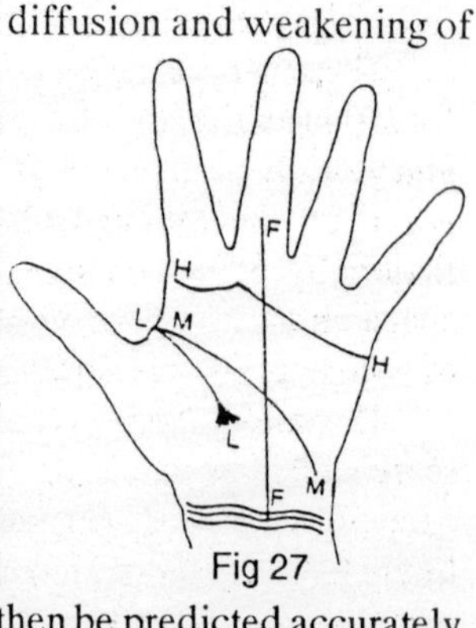

Fig 27

when we examined the same hands after ten or fifteen years, the Line of Life had become faint and indistinct—almost invisible in a portion at a short distance from the bracelet. Lines change, and some marks which may not be visible in a young man's hand today, may be discernible a few years hence.

If you make a habit of looking at your hand daily, you will observe that the lines change—broken ends meet, lines break, islands disappear. Thin lines become thick; narrow ones become broad and broad ones become narrower; new off-shoots appear, and so on.

If a Line of Influence with a bad mark at its commencement and termination point cuts the Line of Life, and ends on the following mounts or lines, the given diseases result:

Mount of Jupiter: apoplexy;

Mount of Saturn: paralysis, if the nails are brittle and fluted, or an accident;

Mount of Apollo: fever;

Mount of Mercury: biliousness, indigestion;

Mount of Mars: blood disorders, surgery, and fever;

Mount of Luna: kidney trouble or disease of the urinary tract;

Line of Heart: heart trouble;

Line of Head: brain trouble;

Line of Mercury: liver trouble.

When the Line of Life is deeply cut and strong upto a particular stage and then gradually tapers, becoming shallower, narrower and then fades away, it indicates death due to a gradual sapping away of vitality. Such persons may suffer for a long time from some chronic disease, and then pass away.

Ending in a Fork: If the Line of Life is strong and forks into two branches—one line running its usual course, and continuing as deeply cut and strong as the Line of Life before the fork—and the other prong, also deeply cut and strong, goes to the Mount of Luna, it shows a great restlessness, and a strong desire to go overseas. But it must be kept in mind that three things are essential for this.

1. Both the prongs should be long, deeply cut, and well marked.
2. The prong continuing from the main Line of Life should

be as deeply cut and well marked as it was before the split.

3. The hand should neither be soft nor flabby. If the hand is soft and flabby, and the Line of Head is sloping downwards, and terminating at the Mount of Luna, the subject will not be painstaking or practical. He will, instead, probably be indolent and lazy, and will not put in sufficient effort to proceed to a foreign country, or establish himself there. He would rather dissipate himself in his own country.

When the Line of Life is divided into two at its termination, and there is a wide space between the two branches, it indicates that the subject is likely to pass his last days in a foreign country. However, the indications given above are for a soft and flabby hand.

If, on the other hand, both the prongs are short, weak, thin, and faded, they indicate the end of life's journey. If there are three or more thin faded prongs instead of two, it is still worse.

Defects

The Line of Life is seldom absent, and is found in most hands. Sometimes, however, only a section of the line is found. Its total absence or its partial presence means that the physical strength and vigour of the subject are at a low ebb, and that the subject lives more on nervous energy than on physical vitality. Another inference drawn is that the subject may fall victim to a sudden fatal illness. Any defect in the Line of Life, such as its absence, or the fact that it is indistinct or short, may be compensated by good Lines of Head and Heart, and a strong thumb.

The Line of Mars, which we shall discuss at greater length later, also acts as a *sister line,* supporting the Line of Life when it is indistinct, short, or absent, or when it shows some defect.

In some hands the Line of Life is short, but the Line of Fate commences from the place where the Line of Life generally ends, and comes upto the Line of Head, or goes even further (Fig. 19-LL, FF). Thus the Line of Fate compensates for the missing part of the Line of Life.

Marks on the Line

Star: A star on the Line of Life (anywhere on the line) is an ominous sign. If there are two stars on the Line of Life in the right hand, or two stars, one in the left hand and the other in the right hand, it indicates sudden death. A star very close to the Line of Life produces the same effect.

Cross: A cross, a cross-bar, or a star (Fig. 28-LL) at the end of the Line of Life is an indication of sudden death. It must be remembered that a cross or a cross-bar in the middle of the Line of Life is only indicative of illness, or an impediment to sound health, or an accident. It is only when either appears at the end of the Line of Life that it indicates sudden death.

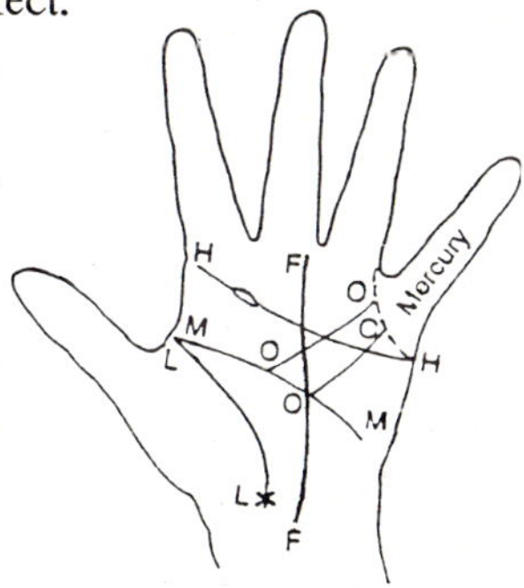

Fig 28

Cross-bars or Cutting Lines: Small, fine lines cutting any major line are called cross-bars or cutting lines. All small lines which cut the Line of Life are prognostications of illness or worry (Fig. 29-LL). If, however, the Line of Fate or the Line of Apollo starts from the Mount of Venus, it will naturally pass over the Line of Life and should not be interpreted as a cross-bar. If many fine lines cross the Line of Life at intervals, the subject is prone to nervous tension and worries, and may suffer from a minor illness or nervous tension extending over a long period of time.

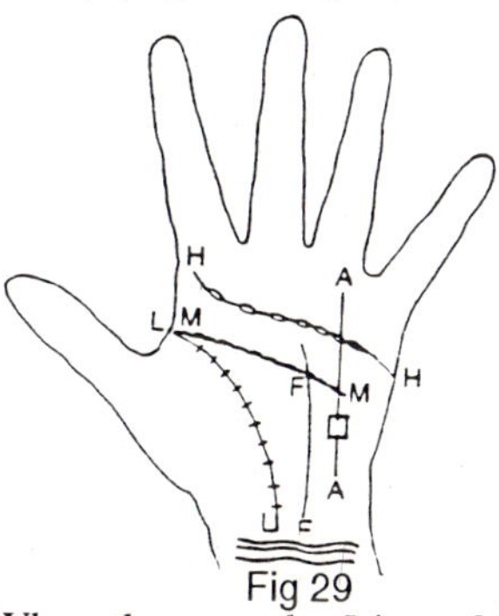

Fig 29

Cross-bars indicate some defect. When they cut the Line of Life, they signify health problems. The magnitude of ill health or illness is gauged from the thickness and length of these cross-bars. The thicker the cross-bar and the deeper the cut, the more serious the illness. The nature of the illness will depend on the particular mount where these cross-bars terminate. A long line cutting across the Lines of Life, Head, and Heart may be indicative of bereavement.

If the cross-bar reaches a mount and ends with a bad mark such as a grille, it is still worse. Some of the diseases pertaining to each mount are given below:

Mount of Jupiter: Diseases arising from an indulgent lifestyle with an excess of food and drink; diseases arising out of an imbalance of phlegm, blood pressure, apoplexy.

Mount of Saturn: Diseases arising due to an imbalance of wind, rheumatism, gout, melancholia, paralysis, accidents—particularly, if a line cutting the Line of Life has a dot at the junction of the line and the cutting line, and it ends in a cross on the Mount of Saturn.

Mount of Apollo: Diseases arising out of an imbalance of bile, heat-stroke, eye trouble. If the cross-bar ends in a dot or spot, or there is a harmful mark on the Line of Heart, the subject could suffer from heart trouble.

Mount of Mercury: Diseases arising from an imbalance of wind, bile or phlegm, or all the three; liver trouble, nervousness, etc.

Mount of Mars: Blood disorders, trouble in the throat and bronchial tubes; diseases arising out of an imbalance of bile.

Mount of Luna: Upper portion—bowel trouble; middle portion—rheumatism; lower portion—malfunctioning of kidneys, or presence of a stone or gravel in the kidneys; trouble connected with ovaries, delivery or monthly periods in the case of ladies; diseases arising out of an imbalance of wind and phlegm.

A line cutting across the Line of Life cannot terminate in the Mount of Venus because the latter is located in the lower portion of the hand, and lines commence from there and do not end there. But since the diseases pertaining to each mount have been specified, we will indicate the diseases pertaining to the Mount of Venus also, in case some unfavourable marks occur there.

Mount of Venus: Diseases arising out of an imbalance of wind and phlegm, urinary and venereal diseases, bladder trouble, spermatorrhoea in case of men, whites in case of women.

If the Line of Life is good and strong and the cross-bars are very fine, the disease will not be serious; but if the Line of Life is weak and the cross-bars are strong, the case is reversed. Look at the condition of the line after it is cut by a cross-bar, and then predict the recovery accordingly.

If the cross-bar cutting the Line of Life terminates at the Line of Head in an island or a deep dot, it signifies mental trouble such as schizophrenia. If the condition of the Line of Life and the Line of Head is worse beyond the place of the cut, the mental trouble will be prolonged. If the cross-bar cutting the Line of Life terminates at the Line of Heart, it indicates some bereavement or heart trouble.

If the cross-bar terminates at the quadrangle and the latter is narrow, it is an indication of asthmatic trouble. A narrow quadrangle is always connected with asthma.

A cross-bar running to a wavy or islanded Line of Mercury, or one on which there is an island shows trouble connected with the stomach and the lungs, respectively. A cross-bar from the Mount of Mars and cutting the Line of Life shows accidents.

Certain indications have been given for cross-bars cutting the Line of Life and ending at the Lines of Head, Heart, or Liver, or on any of the mounts, or Plain of Mars. When these lines commence from a cross, a star, or an island on the Line of Life, or end in a bad mark, the prognostications with regard to illnesses are given below. But when such lines are thin and there is no mark or a cross, either at the commencement or at its termination, it is not to be read as a line indicating illness, but an influence of, or interference by others to the detriment of the subject (for detailed discussion of these cases, please refer to the chapter on the Lines of Influence).

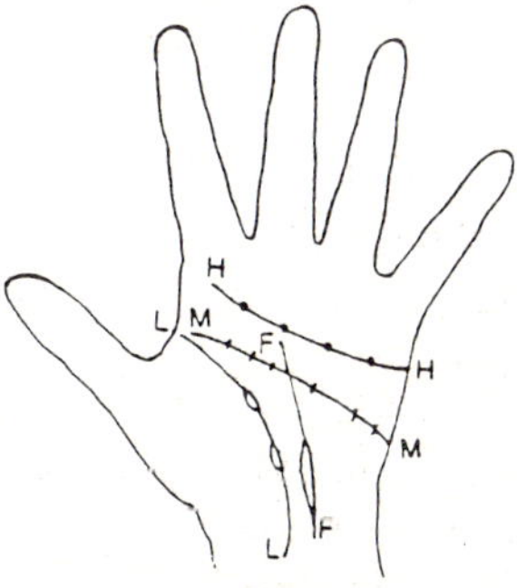

Fig 30

Islands: Islands on the Line of Life show health trouble, according to the size of the island. If there are

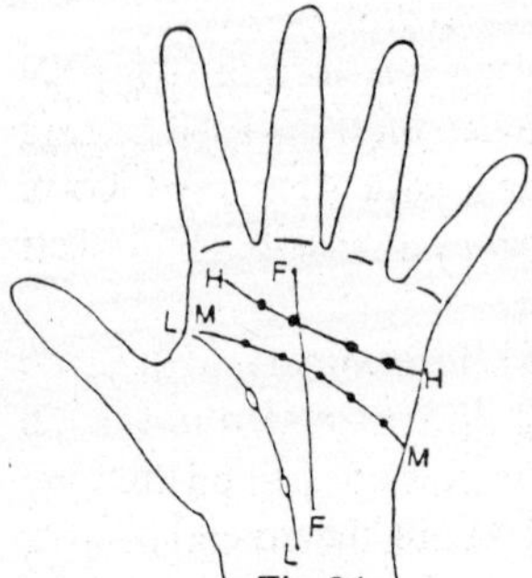

Fig 31

a number of small islands on the Line of Life as well as many fine lines cutting the line, it shows that the native is depressed due to worries and anxieties, and is consequently subject to nervous tension.

If there are islands on the Line of Life, and the Line of Head is cut by small fine lines (Fig. 30-LL, MM), then the subject will suffer from headaches. But if the lines cutting the Line of Head are not fine and make a deep impression on the Line of Head, brain trouble such as schizophrenia is indicated.

An island on the Line of Life and dots on the Line of Head point to brain fever, particularly, if the dots are red (Fig. 31-LL, MM).

An island on the Line of Life and dots on the Line of Heart indicate heart trouble (Fig. 31-LL,HH).

An island on the Line of Life and a wavy Line of Mercury signify diseases of the liver (Fig. 32-LL, NN).

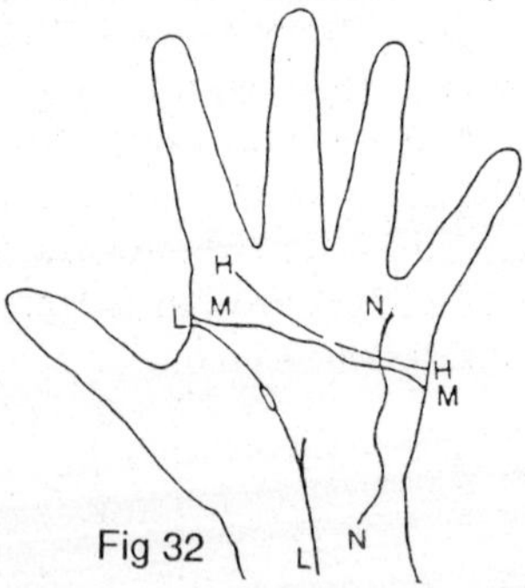

Fig 32

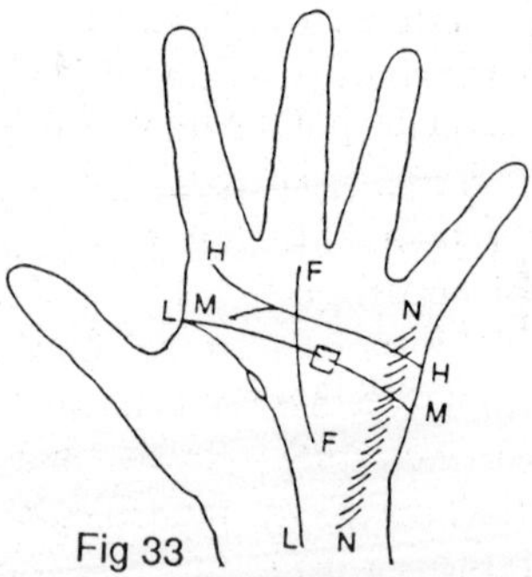

Fig 33

An island on the Line of Life and laddered Line of Health (Fig. 33-LL, NN) show weak digestive powers and loss of appetite.

An island on the Line of Life and a line from the island going to the Mount of Saturn and ending there in a grille is indicative of paralysis, particularly when the nails are brittle and fluted (Fig. 34-LL).

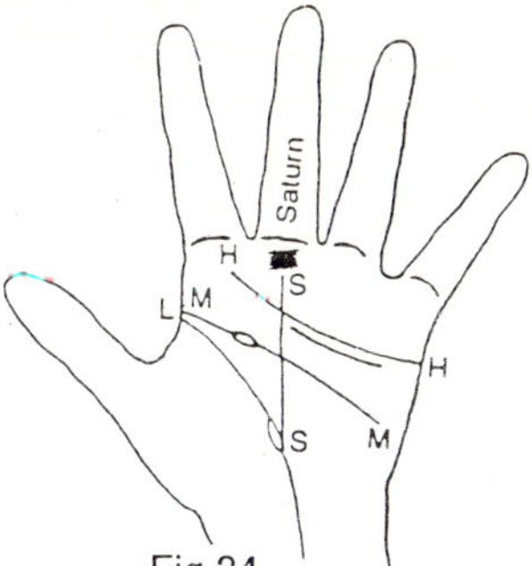

Fig 34

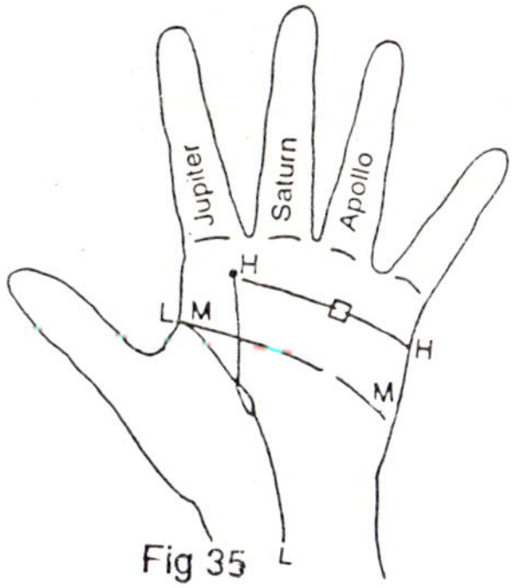

Fig 35

An island on the Line of Life and a line from the island proceeding towards the Mount of Jupiter and ending in a red dot there (Fig. 35-LL) should be read as danger of apoplexy. If there is a grille or cross on the Upper Mount of Mars, then this danger increases because a bad sign on the Mount of Mars shows a hot temper and high blood pressure, which may even result in a stroke.

An island on the Line of Life of a female between the age group of forty and fifty may indicate menopause and some health trouble connected with this change in life. If accompanied by a grille on the lower one-third of the Mount of Luna, it shows weakness connected with menopause. These indications are further confirmed if a line from the island on the Line of Life goes to the grille on the lower one-third of the Mount of Luna, or if there is a star on the junction of the Lines of Head and Mercury.

Breaks in the Line of Life: All breaks in the Line of Life show ill health or illness (Fig. 36-LL). In this connection two things must be noted very carefully.

If the break is in a strong line, that is, the parts before and after the break are strong and deep, it will not have such a negative effect as in a weak, broad, shallow, or indistinct line.

If the break is on both the hands and at the same place, it is more serious.

If besides the break, there are bad marks such as a cross-bar, a cross, or a grille on the Line of Life at the break, and a line goes

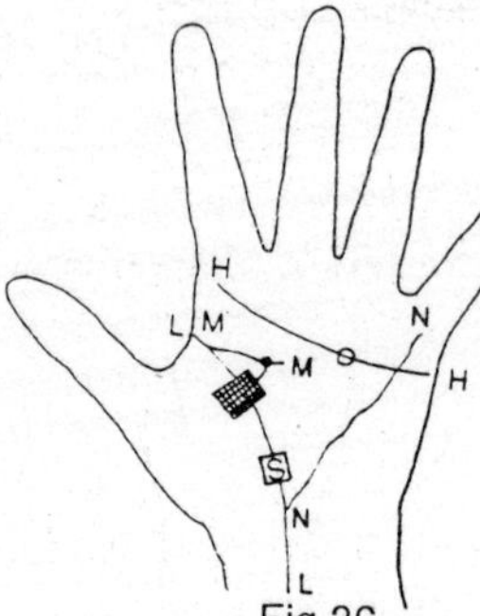

Fig 36

from there to the Lines of Head, Heart, or Mercury, and there is a dot or a cross or a grille, or some such bad marks at the termination of such a line, then the sign is ominous, indicating even death for the subject.

There are, however, four kinds of protections for the break. If any of these is present, the evil effects of the break are lessened. These four protections are

1. A strong Line of Mars, preferably in both the hands, parallel to the Line of Life, and covering the place of the break.
2. If a strong repairing line, however short it may be, covers the space of the break, it helps to protect the life, and the illness is not so severe.
3. A square enclosing the break (Fig. 36-S) which covers the entire broken space.
4. The two parts—before and after the break—overlap each other.

If a hand does not show any indication of sickness, a break in a healthy hand may imply an accident. The severity of the accident will be lessened if one of the four protections (described above) is present. If the break is very wide, it indicates illness and not an accident. If the Line of Life after the break turns back (in the direction from which it was coming), and makes a hook-like appearance, it indicates a very serious illness. A break in the right hand shows illness, but breaks in both the hands (unprotected by a sister line, repair line or square) indicate death. This is so if the break is at the same stage in both the hands.

If the Line of Life shows many thin breaks and gets thinner and indistinct, or broad and shallow, or is full of islands, it shows gradual deterioration of health and the sapping away of vigour and vitality. Islands signify weak health and if there is an island or a chained line after a break, it means that though the subject will recover from the serious illness, attacks of the illness will persist throughout the period covered by the length of the island or the chained line.

Dots on the Line of Life: Dots on the Line of Life (Fig. 37-LL) show some illness or an accident. The nature of the illness will depend on other indications. For example, if two defects, one on the Line of Life and the other on the Line of Head, are connected by a line, it may indicate mental trouble. If there is any connection between the defects in the Lines of Life and Heart, it indicates heart trouble; a connection between the Lines of Life and Mercury denotes liver trouble, nervous ailments, and so on.

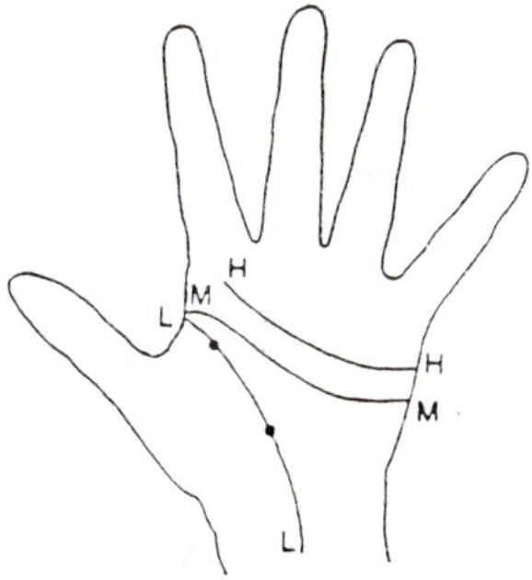

Fig 37

This principle should be applied to other bad signs also. The diseases indicated by the various mounts have been described in a previous section in this chapter, and that diagnosis should be considered when a line cutting the Line of Life goes to a particular mount. This would be especially applicable when there is a defect such as a dot or a cross at the point where a line cuts the Line of Life, and also on the mount at which the cutting line terminates.

Splits in the Line of Life: A Line of Life may split in two directions. A split sloping towards the base of the hand is a bad sign as it diminishes energy. If occuring at a stage in the Line of Life which corresponds to old age, it is sometimes an indication of serious illness or even death, specially if the prong is marked, deep and long.

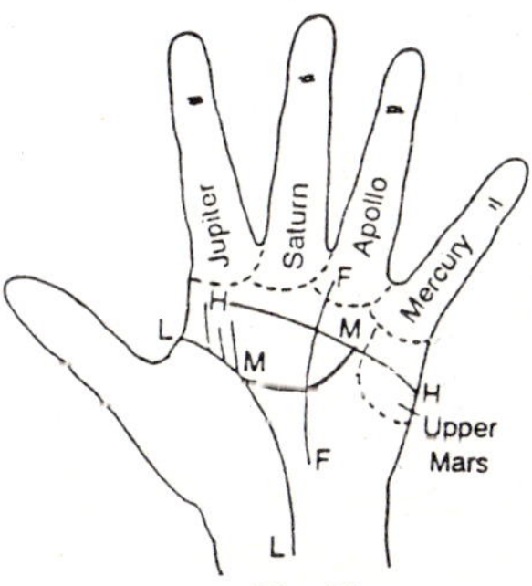

Fig 38

A split in the Line of Life, if appearing as an off-shoot (Fig. 38-LL) of the Line of Life and proceeding towards the Mounts of Jupiter, Saturn, Apollo, Mercury, or Upper Mars, indicates a rise in matters pertaining to the mount towards which it proceeds, or on which it terminates.

Many fine splits going down towards the wrist show a gradual weakening of the constitution.

Some other indications, discussing the nature of diseases, are found in the chapters dealing with the Lines of Head, Heart, and Mercury.

Estimating Age

Fig. 39 gives a rough indication of how age is to be estimated on the Lines of Life, Head, Heart, and Apollo. But lines on all hands differ in length, direction, and curvature. To arrive at an estimation of age on the lines, it is recommended that certain past events in a person's life be identified with specific marks.

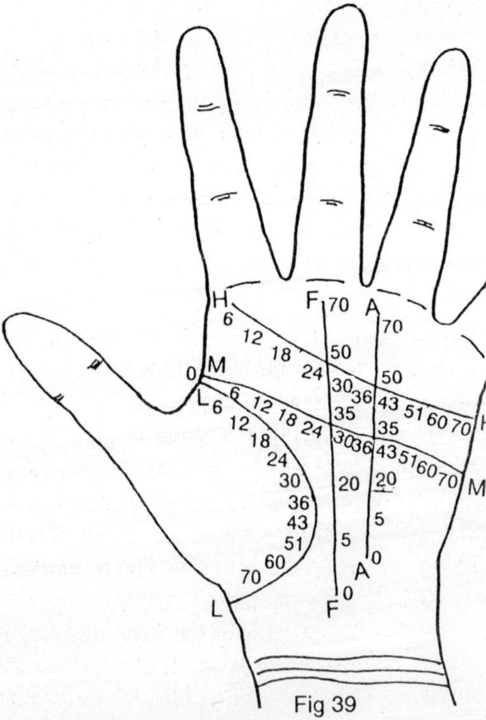

Fig 39

9

Major Lines of the Hand
The Line of Head

The Line of Head or the Line of the Mind, as it is also known, shows the degree of intelligence, grasping power and assiduousness of the subject. These qualities are essential for achieving success in life, whatever career one may pursue. There are many cases of hands which show intelligence and sound judgement, but their quota of success in life has remained very limited, their achievements meagre, and financial gains proportionately low, due to lack of perseverance.

On the other hand, we come across a good Line of Head in many hands, and though many such people are businessmen who have not received any degree from a college or university, yet they possess intelligence, sound judgement, discretion, and perseverance. They have made money and achieved success.

Characteristics

A good Line of Head should be of a healthy pink colour. A slightly yellowish or bluish line shows that the brain is not healthy. A red line indicates too much blood rushing to the head and, as such, is not good.

The Line of Head should be long and clear, going across the palm with a slight tilt to the lower side. A line curving slightly towards the Mount of Luna is also a good line.

A long and clear line, slightly tilted downwards, endows the subject with prudence and steadfastness, and also develops the imagination.

Course of the Line

Commencement: The Line of Head usually commences either at the starting point of the Line of Life (Fig. 40-MM) or at some distance above the starting point of the Line of Life (Fig. 20-MM).

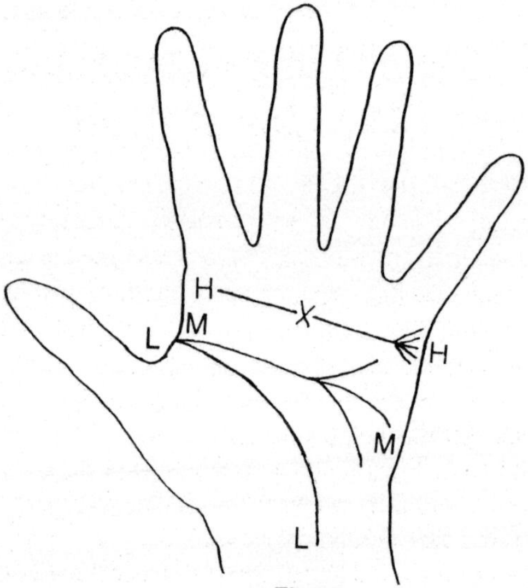

Fig 40

It can also start from the Mount of Venus or the Lower Mount of Mars, and then crossing the Line of Life, comes over to the middle of the palm. In some hands, the Line of Head starts from the Mount of Jupiter (Fig. 41), and in other hands, from under the Mount of Saturn (Fig. 42).

When the Line of Head is joined with the Line of Life at its commencement (Fig. 40-MM), or even when it commences from any other point, it should go across the hand, generally parallel to the base of the fingers. When it starts at the

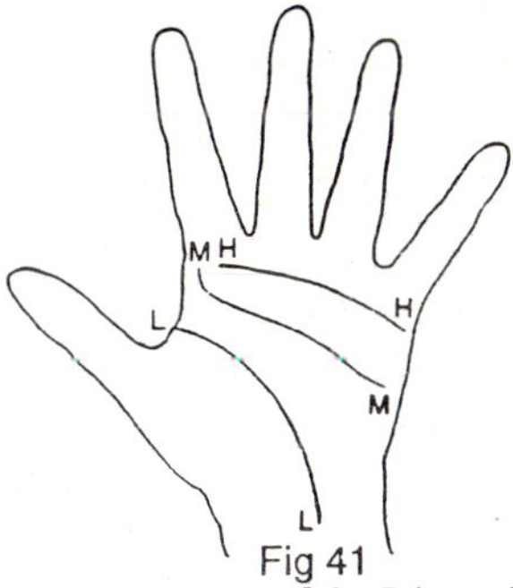

Fig 41

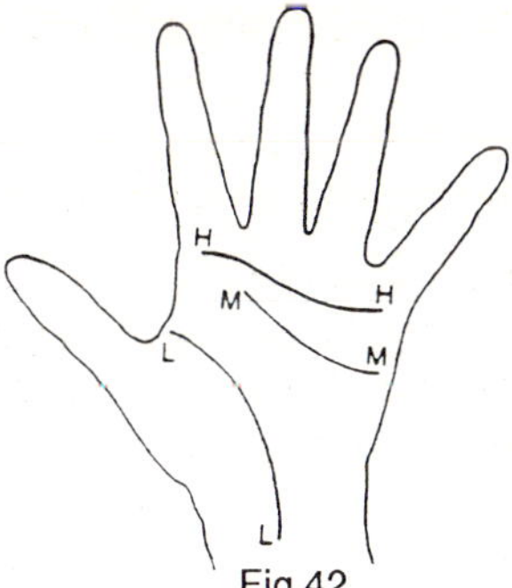

Fig 42

commencement of the Line of Life and is joined with it for some distance, it shows dependence upon others and too much influence of the family; the native lacks adequate self-confidence to translate his will into action. This continues upto the stage it is joined with the Line of Life. At the age (to be reckoned on the Line of Life) when it separates from the Line of Life, the subject becomes more independent and acts in accordance with his own volition. In many hands we have observed that lack of confidence was due to indigent circumstances of the subject, and financial dependence upon the father or other senior members of the family.

A slight gap between the commencing points of the Lines of Life and Head (Fig. 43) shows self-confidence, independence, and a spirit of enterprise, but when the gap between the commencing points of the Lines of Life and Head is excessively wide, the independent streak is far in excess and the subject is prepared to take great risks. This quality in extreme measure makes him imprudent and daring to a degree which is considered a drawback since it involves an imbalance of judgement. While closeness or a narrow gap between the Lines of Life and Head provides caution and reasoning, too wide a gap makes

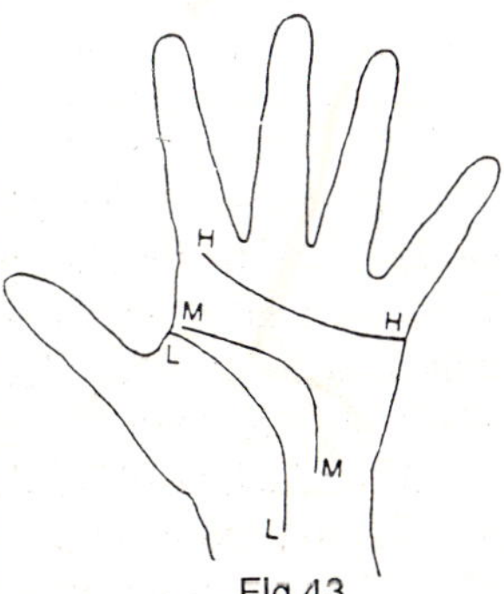

Fig 43

one 'rush in where angels fear to tread.'

In addition the following points should also be remembered:

An elevated Mount of Jupiter gives added optimism. If the Upper Mount of Mars is over-developed, it will make the subject too adventurous. What we want to emphasize is that the gap between the commencing points of the Line of Life and Head should be judged and interpreted along with the elevation of the Mounts of Jupiter and Upper Mars.

If there is a gap between the commencement of the Lines of Life and Head, and there is a badly formed cross between the Lines of Head and Heart, then again the subject is an over-enthusiastic and an optimistic type.

A gap between the commencing points of the Lines of Life and Head is not a good sign if the Mount of Mercury is depressed and the Mounts of Jupiter and Mars are over-developed, because a depressed Mount of Mercury will not bestow sufficient intelligence on the subject to allow him to take advantage of the well-developed Mounts of Jupiter and Mars.

When the Line of Head commences from inside the Mount of Venus or Lower Mars, and proceeds towards the percussion (the Upper Mount of Mars) after cutting the Line of Life, it makes the subject temperamentally erratic and tense (Fig. 21). Such a line, which starts from the Mount of Venus, and cuts across that mount, reduces the Venusian qualities of refinement and co-operation. If it cuts across the Mount of Lower Mars, it will reduce the strength of that mount and the subject's mind will not be very stable and firm.

If the Line of Head starts from the Mount of Jupiter (Fig. 23), it makes the subject proud. The higher up it commences on the Mount of Jupiter, the greater will be the amount of conceit. The individual will be lacking in the spirit of accommodation. If the Line of Heart also lacks sympathy, he will find it difficult to get on with others.

When the Line of Head starts at some distance from the Line of Life, and commences from under the Mount of Saturn (Fig. 22), and particularly if there is an evil mark on it under the Mount of Apollo, it indicates eye trouble in childhood or youth.

If the Line of Head and Heart are both forked at the commencement and two forks proceed upward, it indicates good fortune.

Curvature: If the Line of Head continues in a straight course, the native will be comparatively (Fig. 44-MM) level-headed, but if it slopes towards the Mount of Luna, he will be more imaginative, and hence, less practical in dealing with others.

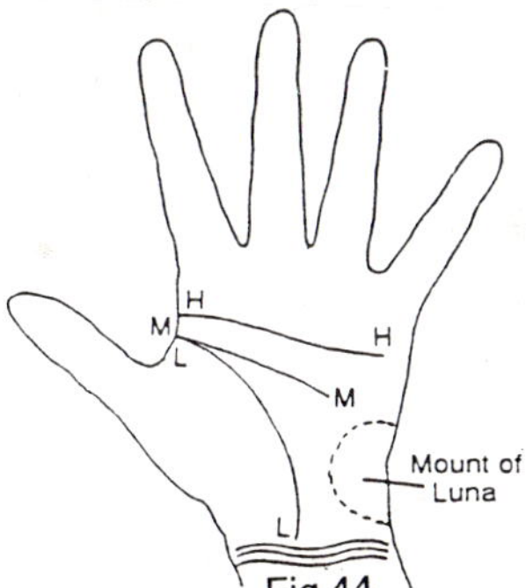

Fig 44

If the first phalange of the thumb shows a dominating nature, the subject's temperament will stand in the way of his being amiable to others.

The normal position of the line is across the palm (Fig. 45-MM). It is good if it rises slightly and then goes across the palm. While going straight across the palm, it can be straight and stiff; straight but slightly inclined to the lower side, that is, towards the Mount of Luna (Fig. 44-MM); straight but slightly inclined to the upper side, that is, towards the Line of Heart.

But in many hands the line is not straight but slightly sloping upwards. In some hands it is markedly sloping downwards but does not reach the Mount of Luna; in others, it reaches the Mount of Luna (Fig. 24-MM); while in still others, after moving upwards for some distance, it becomes as curved as the Line of

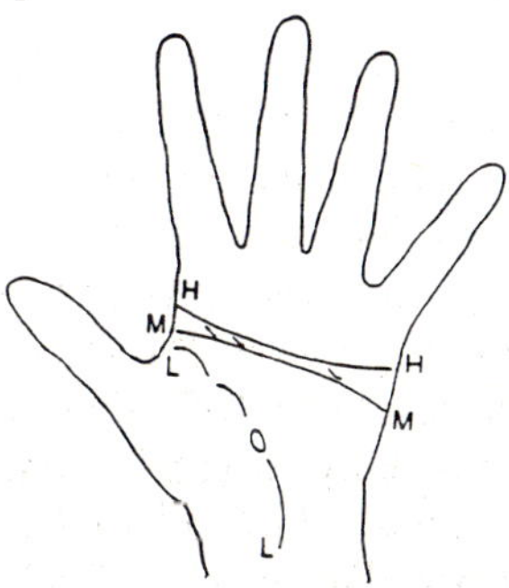

Fig 45

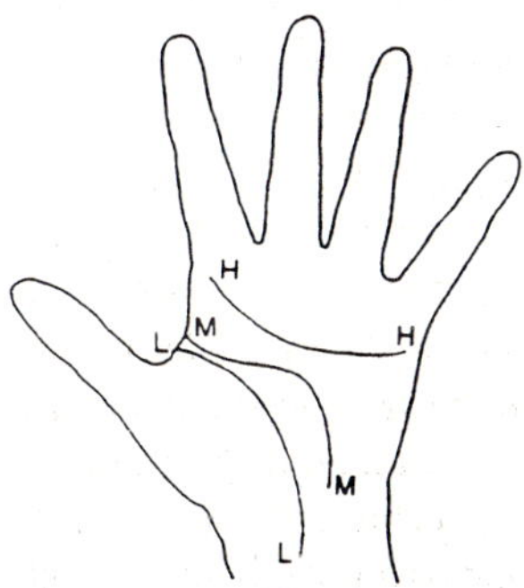

Fig 46

Life, so that in its final stages, it becomes almost parallel to the Line of Life at its termination, though it does not reach so near the bracelet as the Line of Life does (Fig. 46). We shall discuss all these below.

When the line is straight and stiff and reaches the percussion (Fig. 45-MM), it shows greediness. For subjects possessing a line like this, self-interest is the guiding passion in life. It is relevant to note in this connection that it is not a virtue for the line to cross the percussion. It is true that the longer the line, the more powerful the brain. But its contact with the Upper Mount of Mars makes the native strong-headed and vindictive. It also adds to his spirit of aggrandisement, and the native is clever in matters concerning his own self-interest.

When the line is straight but slightly inclined downwards, it provides intelligence and will-power in adequate measure (Fig. 44-MM). At the same time, it also makes the subject generous and more humane. His imagination and emotional development will be of a high order. This line, slightly inclined downwards, increases the distance between the Lines of Head and Heart, and therefore, the subject will be more liberal in outlook as well as in financial matters.

When the line is straight and inclined upwards (Fig. 45-MM), it reduces the space between the Lines of Head and Heart and in this case, the subject becomes miserly. If the quadrangle between the two Lines of Head and Heart becomes very narrow, it may cause asthma.

When the Line of Head is sloping and slightly curved downwards, the subject has a good imagination (Fig. 19-MM). People with a good imagination are successful in fields where imagination is required, such as in artistic pursuits; while people with a straight line are successful in the pure sciences.

When the Line of Head slopes excessively towards the Mount of Luna, it shows a surfeit of imagination. The subject lives more in the realm of thought than in the world of action. An excess of imagination also leads to morbidity. In a philosophic or a psychic hand, it may further enhance the philosophical bent or the psychic power. A slight slope would increase the faculty of invention in a spatulate hand, but an excess of it would spoil the practical wisdom and worldly shrewdness in a square or spatulate hand. Imagination is an asset for a conic hand, but an excess may lead to impracticability and melancholia.

A sloping Line of Head reaching the Mount of Luna and ending in a star shows death by drowning. But if it goes right upto the bracelet and ends there in a cross or a star, it shows good luck.

When the sloping line, after travelling a little, runs down in a curve almost parallel to the Line of Life, it is an evil. It shows a tendency towards self-annihilation on the part of the subject. If the line is found in such a condition in both the hands, it is an indication that the subject will probably commit suicide.

Sister Line: A sister line to the Line of Head shows inheritance (Fig. 26-MM). A double Line of Head also indicates the same thing. It shows a fine intelligence as well. Generally, people have only one Line of Head. A double line is rarely found, and it is so called when both the lines are equally prominent, making it difficult to distinguish between the main line and the sister line. But when there is a long line and another short line running parallel to it, the latter is called a sister line.

Forked at the Beginning: If the Line of Head is forked shortly after its commencement, with one prong going towards the Mount of Jupiter, it is good. But if, of the two prongs, one is straight, and the other proceeds downwards and merges with the Line of Life, it should be assessed as if the Line of Head is joined with the Line of Life.

If the Lines of Head and Heart both have forks, one fork of each of these going upwards, it shows good fortune.

Off-shoots of the Line: All off-shoots going up in the direction of the fingers (Fig. 47) are good, while all off-shoots going downwards in the direction of the wrist are bad.

If an off-shoot starts from the Line of Head and proceeds to the Mount of Jupiter, it indicates success. The general indications of a star on the line have been earlier described as unfavourable, but this description does not hold good if the star is on the Mount

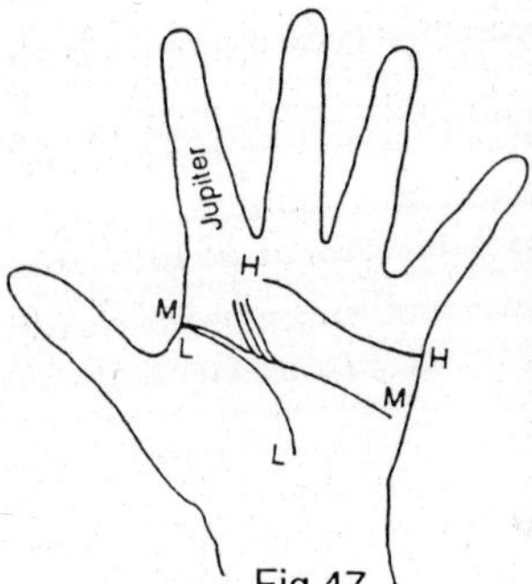

Fig 47

of Jupiter. An off-shoot from the Line of Head terminating on the Mount of Jupiter, with a star at the end of the off-shoot, indicates success. If there is no star at the termination of the off-shoot, and the off-shoot reaches the base of the first finger, it shows high ambition. If the off-shoot, while proceeding to the Mount of Jupiter, is cut by a bar, or if there is a cross on the Mount of Jupiter at the point at which the off-shoot ends, it indicates failure. The age of success (in case of the off-shoot terminating in a star) and failure (in case of the off-shoot ending in a bar or cross) has to be read on the Line of Head, where the off-shoot starts.

If the off-shoot reaches high up on the Mount of Jupiter and there is a cross on the first bracelet, it shows an influx of wealth.

If the off-shoot reaches the Mount of Jupiter, and then turns to the Mount of Saturn, it shows that pride (Mount of Jupiter) has turned into a false ego (Mount of Saturn), or religiousness (Jupiter) into fanaticism (Saturn).

Several off-shoots from the Line of Head reaching the Mount of Jupiter show that the native's ambitions will be fulfilled and that he will be successful.

Any of the branches or off-shoots reaching the Mount of Saturn confer saturnine qualities or morbidity on the subject. Even if the other general indications of the hand are good, the subject will be mentally preoccupied with saturnine inclinations, such as philosophy, occultism, etc. Those who are not inclined towards mental occupations, however, will be successful in fields associated with agriculture, mines, minerals, oils, etc.

The off-shoots from the Line of Head proceeding towards the Mount of Apollo show

- Wealth, if the Line of Fate is good and strong;
- Success in art, if the hand is conical in shape.

The off-shoots from the Line of Head proceeding towards the Mount of Mercury (Fig. 28-MM and 00) indicate an inventive faculty and success; if combined with a good Line of Fate, the subject is likely to earn money through trade and commerce.

Off-shoots starting from the Line of Head and going downwards towards the wrists are evil. They indicate a depletion of mental power.

A line starting from the point where the Line of Fate crosses the Line of Head, and proceeding towards the Mount of Jupiter with a star at the termination, denotes excessive pride.

Generally, an off-shoot starting from the Line of Head and moving upwards towards the palm indicates success due to mental efforts (Fig. 45-MM).

Termination: When the Line of Head commences and proceeds normally, but terminates halfway (Fig. 36 M M) under the Mount of Saturn, it means premature termination of brain power or an early death. Death may be caused by some disease connected with the brain. If the Mounts of Apollo, Jupiter, and Mercury are undeveloped, it indicates stupidity; if the Mount of Mars is also underdeveloped, then it shows a lack of mental courage.

If the line continues its normal course till below the Mount of Saturn and then turns at a right angle (or an almost right angle) and goes to the Mount of Saturn (Fig. 48-MM), it means an injury to the head or the brain. If, on turning towards the Mount of Saturn it does not cross the Line of Heart, the injury is not so serious as when it crosses the Line of Heart and goes deep into the Mount of Saturn.

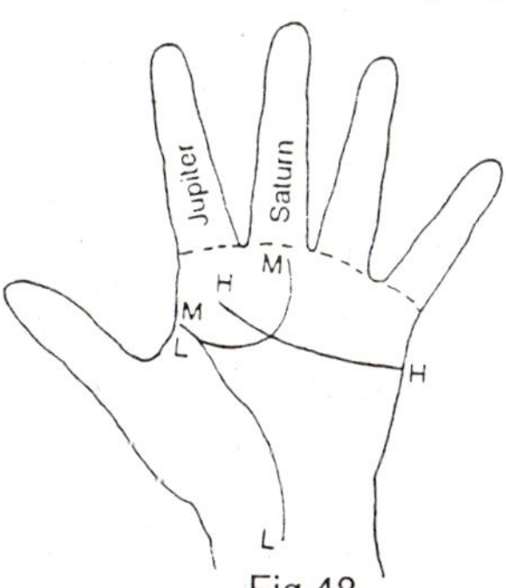

Fig 48

If the line stops just before touching the Line of Fate, it indicates a miserable life. If, in addition, there is a cross at the end of such a Line of Head, it indicates a premature death.

If, after proceeding in its usual course, it turns upwards and turns into a hook on the Upper Mount of Mars, it illustrates vanity and a heightened ego.

If the line proceeds normally about three-quarters of its length, and then turns to the Mount of Apollo and ends there, it shows a strong love for and an inclination towards the fine arts. If this line cuts the Line of Heart on its way to the Mount of Apollo, it dissipates the good influence of the Line of Heart (since the cutting of a line is not good). If the line proceeds towards the Mount of Apollo, but stops short of crossing the Line of Heart, then the subject will be successful in the field of arts. If general indications such as a square or a spatulate hand or a square palm (fingers not pointed) show that the subject is not inclined towards the arts, or has no capacity to win laurels in that field, the turning of the Line of Head towards the Mount of Apollo, and its termination before crossing the Line of Heart indicate acquisition of wealth with comparatively less effort. The native may also gain money by dealing in works of art.

If instead of proceeding towards the Mount of Apollo, the line turns towards the junction of Mounts of Apollo and Mercury, but does not cross the Line of Heart (Fig. 38-MM), it denotes success in art through scientific methods.

If the line turns towards the Mount of Mercury and touches the Line of Heart, it indicates mental weakness or brain trouble. But if it does not touch the Line of Heart, the native will be gifted with the art of mimicry in speech, dress, acting, writing, authorship, etc. If the line goes up to the Mount of Mercury and terminates there, it bestows the mercurial qualities of tact, diplomacy, good expression, and a bargaining power on the subject. A bad hand may show duplicity and a cunning nature.

Line of Head Ending in a Fork: The Line of Head, at times, ends in a fork (Fig. 49-MM). In some hands the two prongs are not equally strong, while in others, both the prongs are of equal length and equal strength. It is generally a good sign for the Line of Head to end in a fork. If the fork is a small one, it adds to the power of a healthy imagination.

If, however, the palm is thick and soft, the fork indicates indolence and love for gross pleasure, with the subject succumbing easily to temptations. If, in addition, will-power is lacking (as in persons having a short thumb), and other indications point to a voluptuous nature, the fork at the termination of the Line of Head may indicate an imagination which may be put to wrong use such as deceiving others. If one of the prongs is straight, and the other is too long and goes well down on to the Mount of Luna, the subject will be highly imaginative and, therefore, more creative. It is reiterated that any connection between the Line of Head and the Mount of Luna signifies more than normal imagination, and that a long prong inclining towards the Mount of Luna may also be helpful in making good money.

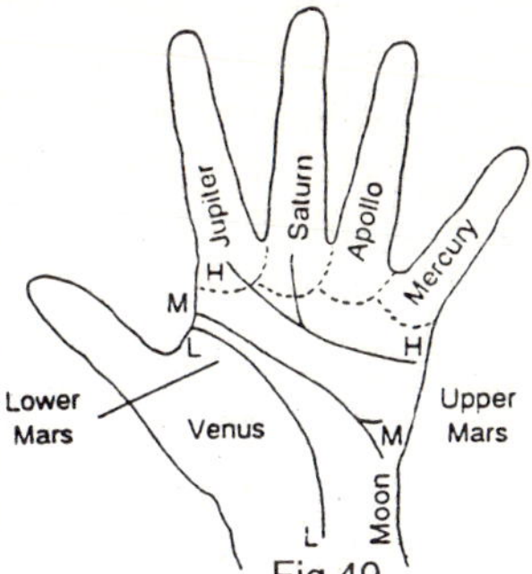

Fig 49

The straight prong contributes to making money by honourable means. A small prong on the Mount of Luna may make one a good diplomat if the finger and the Mount of Mercury are strong.

If, at the termination, the Line of Head splits into two forks, with one prong proceeding towards the Mount of Mercury, it shows psychic powers (due to the prong on the Mount of Luna) and the ability for clever management of business (due to the other prong going on to the Mount of Mercury). A person with a hand like that will be unscrupulous in the matter of earning money. But if it so happens that one prong does not reach the Mount of Luna, and the other does not go to the Mount of Mercury but stops after touching the Line of Heart, the subject's sphere of imagination will be confined to those he loves, and he will make any sacrifices for them.

If the Line of Head ends in a trident (Fig. 40-MM)—one prong being normal and straight, the other reaching the Mount of Luna, and the third one stretching up to the Mount of Mercury—then the native will be endowed with intelligence, imagination, and business acumen, and he will be able to use his artistic talent in a commercial way.

When the Line of Head reaches the Mount of Luna and splits into a fork, with both the prongs remaining on the Mount of Luna itself, it indicates that the subject has an overactive imagination. If other indications are good, the subject may turn out to be a great artist, a poet, or an author, but in a weak hand it shows an imbalance in the power of imagination.

Defects

We have described the normal course of the Line of Head. The line is deemed defective when it has any of the following characteristics:

It must be remembered that a straight line of pinkish colour, uniformly deep throughout its course, is considered good; but if the line does not show the above characteristics and is wavy, uneven, and discoloured, it shows that the physical characteristics of the brain are not healthy, and the temperament is nervous and bilious; the mind lacks strength and vigour. The native will also not be liberal with his money.

If the line is not pinkish but pale; if instead of being a fine deep line, it is broad and chained (Fig. 29-MM); if the Mount of Apollo is underdeveloped; and if the hand is hard, then the native's mental powers will be at a low ebb, both in grasping and in executing intellectual projects.

If the line is long but faint, and the Mount of Mercury is well-developed, it indicates treachery. It is emphasized that a combination of a good Line of Head and a well-developed Mount of Mercury is an asset; but when the line is faint, it debases the intellect by putting it to wrong purposes.

When the Line of Head is deep and red, it shows nervous strain and a tendency to blood pressure.

If the line is very thin or short (Fig. 36-MM) and the Line of Liver is not good (Fig. 36-NN), it denotes a sluggish liver causing headaches or indigestion.

If the line is wavy (Fig. 32-MM) and travels upto the Line of Heart, under the Mounts of Apollo or Mercury, and there are unfavourable marks on the Mount of Luna, it indicates an unsound mind or madness.

If the line is poor, that is, small and indistinct, and the Line of Heart is absent, and the Line of Health is badly broken at several places or is wavy, it indicates that the subject is lacking in mental ability and in warmth of feelings. If the line is small and indistinct, and if the thumb is very small, and the hand is very soft or flabby, the subject is a congenital idiot.

If the line is formed of small islands and the nails are curved, that is, having a convex appearance and not being firm in the flesh, the subject may be afflicted with paralysis.

A short Line of Head and a depressed Mount of Mercury mean a lack of intelligence.

A short Line of Head starting from under the Mount of Saturn indicates eye trouble.

A short Line of Head terminating before it reaches the Line of Fate, with a cross at the end of it, indicates an early death.

A knotty Line of Head shows that the native is cruel-hearted, and if the line proceeds towards the Upper Mount of Mars, and if the first phalange of the thumb is heavy, the native may even murder his adversary.

Marks on the Line

Square: A square on the Line of Head has a protective influence. It saves the subject from the evil effects of a break or a cross on the line, if the break or the cross is enclosed by the square (Fig. 33-MM). If there is a square and there is no ill mark enclosed by it—that is, the portion of the line enclosed by the square is good and without any evil mark—even then it acts as a protective force during that period of life. If the subject meets with an accident or misfortune during that period of life (the age being reckoned on the Line of Head), he will get away without being hurt in any manner.

Island: An island on the Line of Head is a major defect (Fig. 34-MM). It has a particularly harmful effect if the space covered by the island is dark and depressed. The native may suffer from a serious head injury, or the normal functioning of the brain may be impaired during the age (to be reckoned on the Line of Head) covered by the island. If the course of the line is in a good state afterwards, then the native will recover completely and regain his mental powers. But if the condition of the line after the island is not so good, the native will continue to have some disability even after he crosses the age covered by the island.

An island also shows chronic neuralgia. If, along with the island on the Line of Head, the Line of Health, at the point of its crossing the Line of Head, is red, then it indicates an improper functioning of the brain due to a bad liver. If the island on the Line of Head is under the Mount of Saturn, it denotes deafness.

Several islands on the line may indicate brain trouble due to vigorous intellectual work, or may be a sign of repeated mental trouble. A large island at the end indicates intestinal trouble. It is said that Mars governs heat. It is the heat inside the stomach called *Jatharagni* (the fire inside the stomach in Hindu texts) which helps the digestion of food, and any evil mark on the Upper Mount of Mars impairs the digestive powers. The liver governs the secretion of the bile. So a combination of harmful traits on the Lines of Health and Head impair the mental powers due to the imperfect functioning of the liver; while a combination of bad marks on the Line of Head and the Upper Mount of Mars impairs the intestines.

When the Line of Head reaches the Mount of Luna and an island is formed on the line there, then also, it shows an impaired functioning of the intestines or kidneys. The kidneys and the intestines are more or less in the same region in the human body.

Cross-bars: Cross-bars on the Line of Head (Fig.30-MM) show worries or headaches. The same is indicated when there are capillary lines emanating from the line and proceeding downwards. If the Line of Head is sloping and moves down to the Mount of Luna, and the bars cutting the Line of Head are deep and many, then it is an indication of insanity.

Break: A break is a defect and may indicate an injury to the head. Many small breaks indicate headaches.

If there is a repair line, or if the break is enclosed by a square (Fig. 33-MM), or if the two parts of the broken line overlap each other, the seriousness of the defect due to the break is mitigated. If there is no repair line or any other protection; if the line is broken into small pieces; if there are short nails and a cross in the triangle (between the Lines of Head, Life, and Health), the native will be prone to attacks of epilepsy.

If the break occurs under the Mount of Saturn, and the Line of Head is sloping towards the Mount of Luna, and runs almost parallel at that stage with the Line of Life, then the indication is that of insanity. However, to determine the intensity of brain trouble, the other hand must also be examined.

A break under the Mount of Saturn with no protection (sister line, repair line, square, or the two parts overlapping) in both the hands, and the Line of Life terminating at the corresponding age, indicate death in an ignoble manner. A cross in the triangle, that is, between the Lines of Life and Head, indicates death by hanging.

Defects on the Line of Head under the Mount of Saturn also indicate an injury to the leg. In Hindu mythology, there is a story that when Saturn was a boy, he was scolded by his stepmother. Enraged by this, he lifted his leg and wanted to hit his stepmother, upon which, she cursed him and made him lame. Astrologically, and in palmistry, Saturn is connected with lameness.

A defect such as a break on the line under the Mount of Apollo signifies a loss of vision (Fig. 35-MM). The native may also suffer from sunstroke or hydrophobia.

In a female hand, if the Line of Head is broken where it meets the Line of Fate, and a line starting from the Line of Heart goes down and crosses the Line of Fate, it denotes widowhood or death of a beloved.

If there is a perfect triangle formed by the Lines of Life, Head, and Health, and there is a cross on the Line of Head before it meets the Line of Health, it shows an injury to the head or some accident. If, in the above case, the Line of Head is wavy and has a break, and there is a cross on the point of the break, the accident may be fatal.

Star: A star on the Line of Head shows an injury to the head. If the star is found on the same place on the Line of Head in both the hands, it indicates death.

In a female hand, if there is a star on the junction of the Lines of Head and Health, it shows health troubles during pregnancy; it also indicates that she may be barren.

Circle: A circle on the Line of Head, particularly under the Mount of Apollo, and a cross on the Line of Health will mean a loss of vision.

Triangle: A triangle on the Line of Head is indicative of success—whether it lies in the sphere of Jupiter, Saturn, Apollo, or Mercury should be judged according to the position occupied by the triangle on one or the other mount—but it should be on the Line of Head.

Spots on the Line

A deep but colourless dot on the line denotes mental and nervous trouble, but if the dot is white it improves the mental faculty. The native may make some invention if the hand and fingers are spatulate.

Contrary to the general principles, if there are small bars on the Line of Heart and white spots on the Line of Head, the native will have a literary bent of mind. If there are white spots on the Line of Head, under the Mount of Saturn, then the subject will be successful in intellectual pursuits. But if the white spots on the Line of Head are under the Mount of Mercury, success will lie in the area of natural sciences.

While the white spots have been described as good, dark or blue spots are considered harmful. If the Lines of Life and Head are coloured and narrow, and there are dark, blue or black spots on the Line of Head, enteric fever or a similar illness is indicated. But if black spots are found on the Line of Head, and if the Line of Life is forked at the commencement, the indications point to a disease of the mind.

A blue spot on the Line of Head before it touches the Line of Health, combined with a thick upper phalange of the thumb, and an overdeveloped Mount of Mars, show a murderous attitude. The overdeveloped Upper Mount of Mars reflects an excess of anger and courage. The thick and clubbed first phalange of the thumb shows strong will-power and brutality.

When they combine with a bluish spot on the Line of Head, they indicate that the native has no control over his brutish passions, and if the Line of Head, while ascending the Mount of Mars, goes well up to the percussion, a revengeful nature and vindictiveness is indicated.

If the Line of Head is not straight but zig-zag, and the Line of Health is also wavy, and there is a bluish spot on the Line of Health—illnesses such as malaria, indigestion, liver trouble and nervous ailments may trouble the individual.

If a Line of Influence commencing from a star on the Mount of Venus comes to the Line of Head, and there is a black spot on the Line of Head where the Line of Influence ends, it implies a great mental shock due to a bereavement.

If a Line of Influence begins from the lower part of the Mount of Venus or from the Line of Life, and proceeds towards the mount or the line, and if there are bad marks, both at the commencement and the termination of that Line of Influence, and if black spots are also found on the Line of Head—then it indicates that the subject will suffer from attacks of delirium.

If there are black spots on the Line of Head, and if the Mount of

Apollo is excessively developed, loss of vision is denoted;
Mercury is overdeveloped, nervous trouble may be expected;
Saturn is overdeveloped, the subject will have tooth trouble;
Venus is overdeveloped, deafness may afflict the native.

We could go on elaborating on the bad effects produced by dark, bluish, or blackish spots on the Line of Head, but we prefer to conclude with the final remark that, except for white spots, all coloured spots on the Line of Head are harmful.

NOTE: To estimate age on the Line of Head, see Fig. 39.

10

Major Lines of the Hand
The Line of Heart

The Line of Heart is the key to the emotional background of an individual. It discloses how a person behaves towards those he loves and why; it determines the manner in which he accepts or rejects love. Relationships with the opposite sex, parents, family, and friends are influenced by the Line of Heart.

Characteristics

A broad, long, and deep Line of Heart is good. Unlike the Line of Head which is considered good if deep and narrow, the Line of Heart should not be narrow. A long and clear line indicates lasting affection.

The Line of Heart should be of a pinkish colour. If its colour is white, yellow, or very red, it indicates that the heart is not functioning in a healthy manner. A white line shows that the heart does not pump in a sufficient amount of blood. A yellow line indicates a sluggish liver. A pale, short, and wide line symbolises heart disease due to a bad liver. A very red line may suggest the possibility of thrombosis and violence in love due to too much heat in the passion.

Course of the Line

Commencement: The Line of Heart runs under the Mounts of Jupiter, Saturn, Apollo, and Mercury. Its commencing points are usually any of the following:

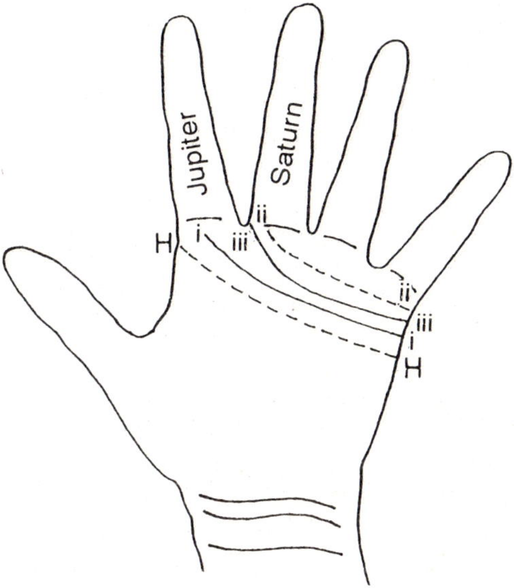

Fig 50

1. From the base of the first finger (Fig. 50—i-i);
2. From the Mount of Jupiter (Fig. 15-HH);
3. From the base of the second finger (Fig. 50–ii-ii);
4. From the Mount of Saturn (Fig. 50–iii-iii); and
5. From the base of the Mount of Saturn (Fig. 20-HH).

The commencing point is important, for the Mount of Jupiter is interpreted as idealism in love, while the Mount of Saturn is connected with sensuousness. It must be remembered that the greater the area it covers on the Mount of Jupiter or that of Saturn, the more the qualities of that mount will it inherit. Thus when it starts at thc the base of the first finger, love will be refined and idealistic, and its warmth will be maximum. When it starts at the Mount of Jupiter, all these qualities will be there, but not in such an abundant measure as in the former case. And when it stems from under the Mount of Jupiter but does not touch the mount, the qualities of love and idealism will be there because the commencing point is not on the Mount of Jupiter, but lies as if 'under the shadow of Jupiter'.

This analogy should be extended to the commencement of the line on the Mount of Saturn.

The larger the area the Line of Heart covers on the Mount of Saturn, the more sensuous will the subject be. The same will be applicable if the line originates from under the Mount of Saturn, for here, the commencing point will be as if 'under the shadow of the Mount of Saturn'. If the line starts between the Mounts of Jupiter and Saturn, the subject will portray a mixture of ideal love and sensuousness, and will follow an in-between path in his affections, giving neither much happiness nor much unhappiness.

There are certain other characteristics connected with the commencing point.

- Whenever a major line of the hand goes on to the third phalange of the finger, it is considered a disadvantage; and if the line commences on the third phalange on the Jupiter finger, there are hurdles in the way of success due to emotions and sentiments standing between the person and his goal.

- When the Line of Heart commences from the third phalange of the Saturn finger, it also shows morbidity arising from an emotional relationship, or separation from a loved one.

A short Line of Heart starting from under the Mount of Saturn (Fig. 20-HH) indicates curtailment of longevity; more sensuality in love than sincerity; and early death if there is a cross on the Line of Head.

If the line starts at the roots between the first and second finger (Fig. 21-HH), the feelings of love and passion will be there (Jupiter finger–love; Saturn finger–passion) but they will remain suppressed and the subject's life will be hard and full of struggle.

The usual places from where the Line of Heart commences have been described above. Let us now look at the other commencing points of the Line of Heart.

If it is joined to the Lines of Life and Head at the commencement (Fig. 51-LL, MM, and HH), it indicates sudden death due to thrombosis in the head or heart, paralysis, heart failure, or accident–particularly so, if there is a cross on the Line of Head.

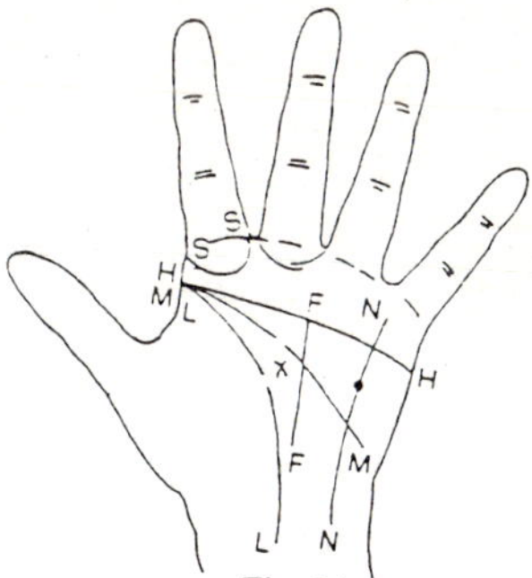

Fig 51

If one long prong from the Line of Heart goes to the Mount of Jupiter and is cut there by a small bar, it indicates a passionate attachment to someone and sorrow resulting from a failure to win over the object of his affections (Fig. 22-HH).

If the Line of Heart has a fork at the commencement, and the Line of Head ends in a fork, one prong continuing the natural course of the Line of Head, while the other is long and sloping and goes to the Mount of Luna, it indicates a love which remains strong and deep (Fig. 52-LL, MM, and HH).

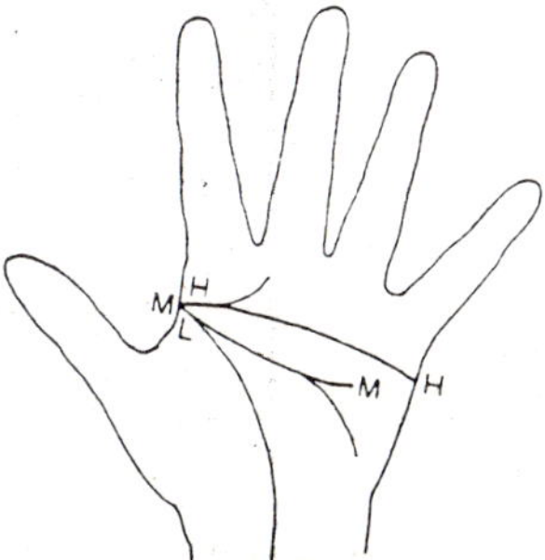

Fig 52

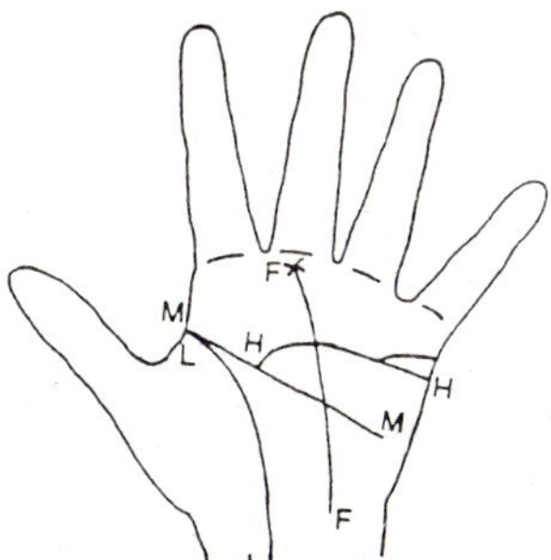

Fig 53

If the Line of Heart is joined to the Line of Head under the Mount of Saturn (Fig. 53-HH, MM), it signifies calamity due to blind love. If it is so in both the hands, it means sudden death.

If under the above condition, the Line of Heart is cut by a bar, it shows grief. The beloved may forsake the subject or prove unworthy of the love given (Fig. 53-HH).

Commencing with a Fork: If the Line of Heart has two forks at its commencement, both forks being on the Mount of Jupiter (Fig. 23-HH), it adds to idealism in love; if there are three prongs instead of two, all on the Mount of Jupiter, it is still better. If the Line of Heart makes a kind of Solomon's ring (Fig. 29-HH) and then proceeds straight towards the percussion under the Mount of Mercury, it points to jealousy and love for occultism.

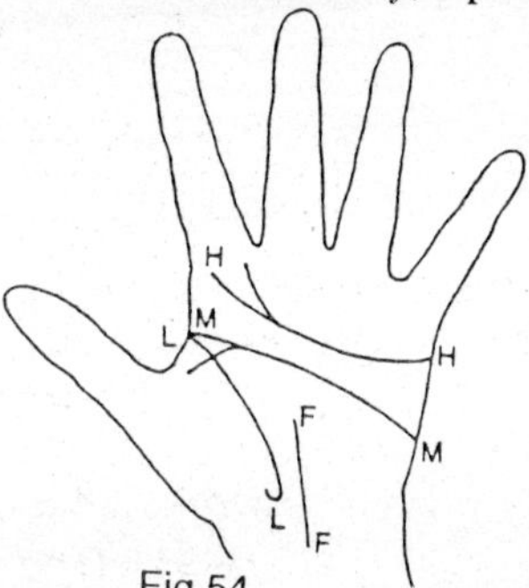

Fig 54

If the line starts with two prongs, one going upwards to the Mount of Jupiter, and the other downwards reaching the Line of Head but not touching it, it shows happiness from the loved one (Fig. 33-HH). In such a case, if there is also a cross on the Mount of Venus, it is still better.

If one prong of the Line of Heart goes to the Mount of Jupiter and the other to the Mount of Saturn (Fig. 49-HH), or to the junction of the Mounts of Saturn and Jupiter, and a fork from the Line of Head goes down to the Lower Mount of Mars, it shows separation from the loved one (Fig. 54-MM).

If one prong of the Line of Heart goes to the Mount of Jupiter and the other towards the Line of Head, it implies disillusionment in an emotional matter.

If, of the two prongs, one goes to the Mount of Jupiter and the other to a position between the roots of the first and second fingers, it signifies domesticity and love.

Curvature: The Line of Heart may be slightly curved and go towards the percussion (Fig. 55-HH).

It may be straight and go towards the percussion (Fig. 56-HH).

It may get deflected and go higher up towards any of the mounts or lower down towards the Line of Head (Fig. 57-HH).

When it follows a straight course, it is in a natural position; when it moves higher up on the hand and nearer the mounts, it imbibes more of the qualities of the mounts, making the subject more sentimental. However, when the line is lower down than its usual place and, as such nearer to the Line of Head, the sentimental side is not so developed. The Line of Heart being nearer to the Line of Head, the mind controls the heart.

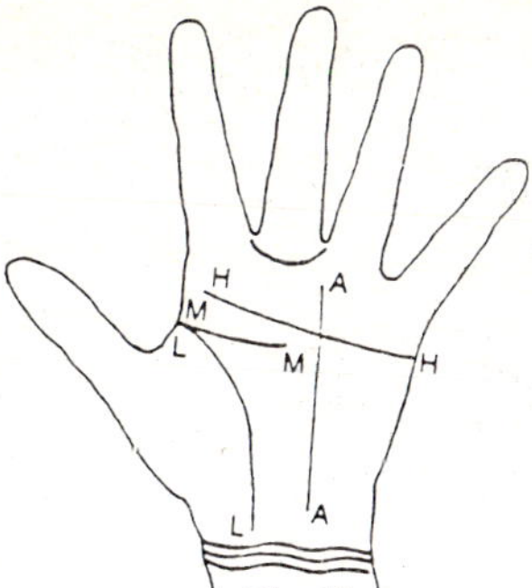

Fig 55

But if the Line of Heart is in its normal position, and the Line of Head is higher up from its normal position and closer to the Line of Heart, it is the heart that controls the head. In both the cases, therefore, the decisive point is which of the two lines–the Lines of Heart and Head–is following the usual course, and which one is not in its usual place.

When the Line of Head is traversing its usual path and the Line of Heart becomes wavy–at some points, coming too near the Line of Head, and at some places, going far from it–the interpretation should be that whenever the Line of Heart draws nearer to the Line of Head, the mind will rule the heart; age should be reckoned on the Line of Heart (Fig. 39). Suppose at this age some indication of a love affair is found, then judging that such an alliance or marriage will not be propitious, the native should not enter into an alliance or should break the engagement. When the Line of Heart is very near the Line of

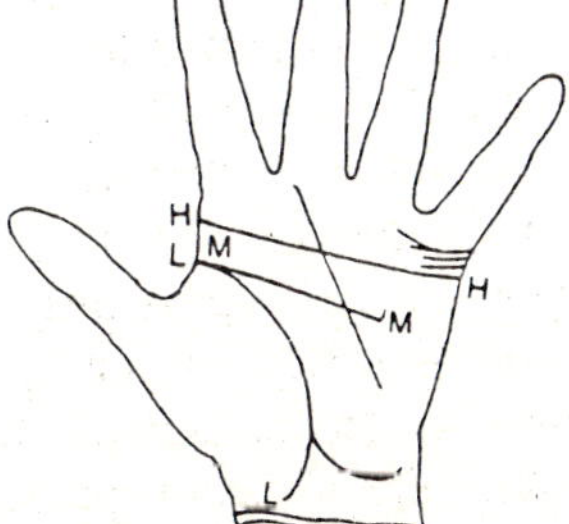

Fig 56

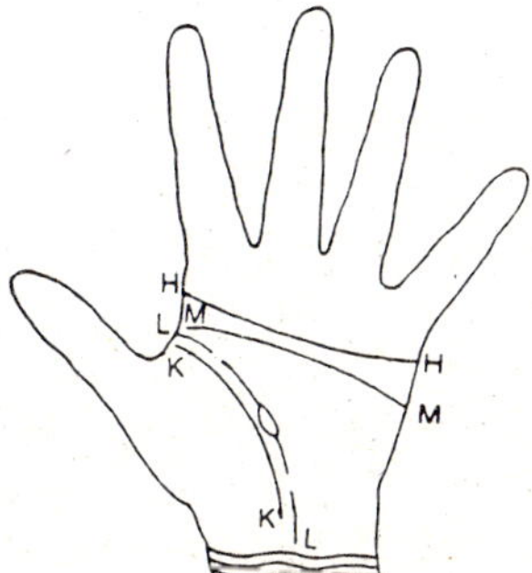

Fig 57

Head (Fig. 55-HH), it indicates that the native is not liberal-hearted, particularly so, if the fingers are smooth. If the Mount of Luna is also excessively developed, it shows duplicity and a cunning nature. This is an example of deflection of the Line of Heart to the lower side (Fig. 57-HH).

If the Line of Heart deflects towards any mount, it should be read as an attraction to, or an attachment with a person represented by that mount. For example, if the Line of Heart deflects to the Mount of Saturn, the attraction will be to a saturnine person. In this way the position of the Line of Heart tells you at what age, and to which type of person the subject (whose hand you are examining) will be attracted.

If the Line of Heart curves downwards, and after cutting the Line of Head, goes down to the Triangle (space between the Lines of Head and Life), it implies serious damage to the mental faculties—high fever accompanied by delirium or death.

Off-shoots: The off-shoots of the Line of Heart are generally not so long as those of the Line of Life. One kind of off-shoot, in the form in which it is found in many hands, is at the commencement. These have already been discussed under the heading 'Forked at the commencement'. Now we shall examine the small thin lines which arise from the Line of Heart. Some palmists have called them *splits*. Others allude to them as branches. Neither of the nomenclatures is really suitable, so we shall call them off-shoots.

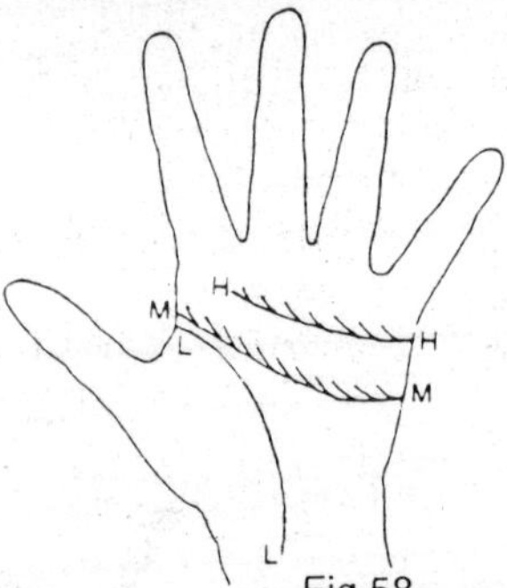

Fig 58

These off-shoots either proceed upwards (Fig. 58-HH) towards the mounts or downwards (Fig. 59-HH) towards the Line of Head. As they are very thin and short lines, it is better to examine them under a magnifying glass.

When they proceed upwards, the sign is good, indicating that the subject will have affinity for the person or work described by the mount towards which the off-shoots proceed.

Each of the four mounts—Jupiter, Saturn, Apollo, and Mercury—represent different types of persons.

A person is called a particular type when his particular mount and finger are well developed. The Mount of Mars, Luna, and Venus have no fingers pertaining to them. The seven types of persons according to the development of the particular mount are as follows:

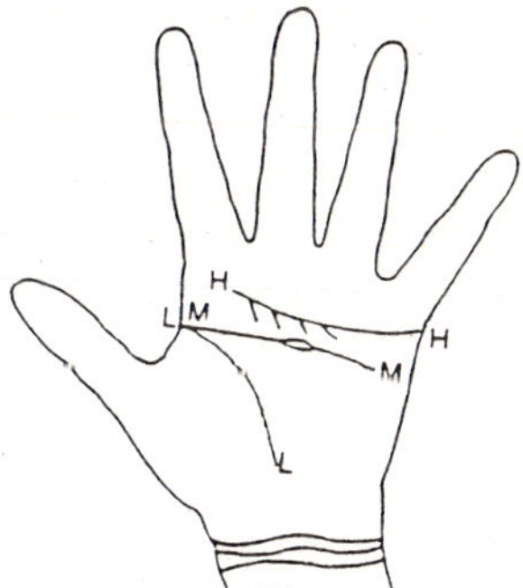

Fig 59

Jupiter: proud, ambitious, rich, religious, robust, fond of eating and drinking.

Saturn: lean and thin, dark, tall, thoughtful, careful. If the phalange is long, the subject will be a scholar in philosophical and occult sciences, with an equal proficiency in exact sciences such as mathematics. If the second phalange of the Saturn finger is proportionately longer, then he is expected to have a love for country life and agriculture. If the third phalange is comparatively long and strong, then the subject will be a miser.

Apollo: the subject will be fond of speculation and gambling. If the Apollo finger is very long, he will be a lover of art. If the first phalange is comparatively long, his appreciation of art will be finer; if the second phalange is strong, he is likely to earn money through art; and if the third phalange is comparatively long, he will be fond of ostentation in dress and entertainment. Apollonians will generally be warm of heart.

Mercury: fond of learning and speaking; versatile in knowledge; a linguist and a good interpreter, provided the first phalange of the Mercury finger is strong. If the second phalange is comparatively strong, the native will excel in the field of science; and if the third phalange is strong, then he will excel in trade and commerce.

Mars: headstrong, courageous, a hard worker, a victor in battles. The native will be energetic.

Luna: indolent; imaginative but lacking the ability to translate ideas into action; a soft body with an excess of protoplasm. The subject will be fond of living near water.

Venus: not tall and with a plump, soft body, fair complexion, narrow forehead, large hips; easily excited by sex; aesthetic.

These guidelines have been provided to determine the various types of persons. The off-shoot commencing from the Line of Heart may not actually travel to the four mounts, but even if it travels in the direction of any of the four mounts, the type of person one would be attracted to can thereby be determined.

So far we have discussed the off-shoots proceeding towards the base of the fingers. But the off-shoots originating from the Line of Heart, and proceeding downwards towards the Line of Head are harmful, and indicate problems about matters connected with the heart.

If an off-shoot from the Line of Heart cuts the Line of Fate or reaches it, and if there is a break in the Line of Fate at that stage, it indicates widowhood. Such an indication in a male hand shows deep sorrow and consequent loss of income. In this case, the age has to be reckoned on the Line of Fate.

Connecting Lines: There are some short lines which are not off-shoots of the Line of Heart but which influence the subject in matters of the heart.

If an off-shoot of the Line of Fate

- proceeds towards the Line of Heart and touches it, marriage or consummation of love affair can be anticipated at that stage;

- proceeds in the direction of the Line of Heart but does not touch it, marriage or consummation of love affair are unlikely;

- cuts the Line of Heart, a love affair will end in disaster.

Several lines, starting from the Line of Heart may proceed towards the Line of Head but not touch it. If these lines are

- under the Mount of Saturn, the subject is susceptible to the influence of members of the opposite sex;

- under the Mount of Apollo, it may be inferred that the subject has a versatile mind.

Several lines, starting from the Line of Life and touching the

Line of Heart denote sorrow and disappointment in the field of love and consequent ill health.

A line starting from the Line of Head and touching the Line of Heart is indicative of a deep attachment.

Termination: Generally the Line of Heart ends in the percussion under the Mount of Mercury (Fig. 56-HH). The longer the line is, the better. But if it is high set (nearer the mounts or over them), it makes one more sentimental. If it is low set (Fig. 55-HH), the native is not easily swayed by emotions. If the line crosses the hand from one side to the other (Fig. 56-HH), then also, the native is very sentimental and loving. However, if the line is too stiff and straight, and the hand is also hard, then the native is not sentimental. If the line is long and there is an overdeveloped Mount of Luna, it indicates love tinged with jealousy.

If the line is faint and poorly formed ending without off-shoots at the end, it indicates loss of reproductive power—sterility in a female hand, and similar effects in a male hand.

If the line ends in the percussion, and if there is a strong Line of Head with the Upper Mount of Mars being well developed, and the first phalange of the thumb being strong, the indication is that the subject is courageous and bold.

If the line goes up to the Mount of Mercury, encircles it and ends at the root of the fourth finger, it shows an inclination towards the occult sciences; if it is accompanied by a good Line of Head, it indicates success therein.

If the line is forked at the termination, one fork following the natural course of the line and the other fork going up to the Mount of Mercury, then the subject is likely to get involved in a clandestine love affair, followed by divorce.

If the line ends in a tassel (Fig. 40-HH) then it means a gradual weakening in the influence of the heart. It also shows a diffusion of emotions into various quarters.

If no fork is formed at the terminal point of the line and the Mount of Venus (Fig. 55-HH) is depleted, and the hand is soft and flabby, then the subject is lacking in maturity and tends to be childish.

Double Line of Heart: A double Line of Heart (Fig. 34-HH) shows intensity in love affairs. It exerts a positive influence when it is long, even and well-marked, and devoid of any harmful signs. In female hands it shows that health will be good and there will be no trouble with regard to the menstruation cycle, the ovaries, or the womb.

Marks on the Line

If the Line of Heart is broad and shallow, it points to weak functioning of the heart. If it is chained, it also shows the same defect. If the line is good, deep-cut, and clear during a certain stage and the rest is defective, then the condition of the heart and its functioning will be normal at the corresponding age (to be reckoned on the Line of Heart) where it is without a blemish; and the action of the heart will be impaired during the age that the line is broad and shallow, or chained. The same principles should be applied to any other marks which are observed on the line.

All defects on the Line of Heart bode ill, but those under the Mount of Apollo are indicative of even greater harm.

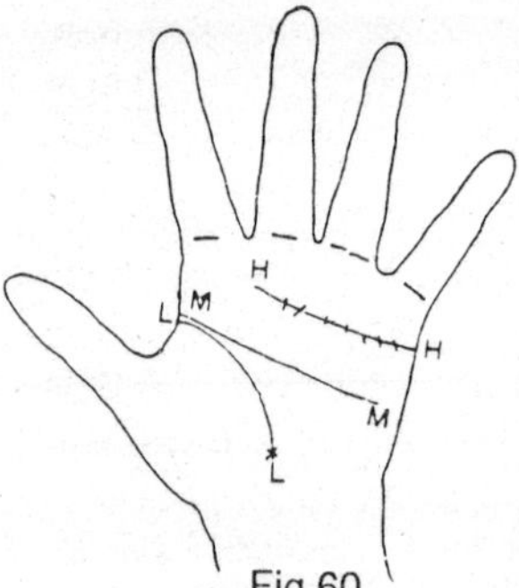

Fig 60

Cross-bars: Cross-bars cutting the line (Fig. 60-HH) show disappointments or worries about the people one loves. Numerous cross-bars indicate that the native will have constant worries or many disappointments in love. They may also denote palpitation of the heart, indicating at the same time that the valves of the heart are not functioning properly.

If one of the prongs of a cross on the Mount of Mercury cuts the Line of Heart, it signifies failure in business.

Islands: An island on the Line of Heart (Fig. 28-HH) is a serious defect. It may show suffering due to entanglement in a love affair or heart disease. Numerous small islands (Fig. 29-HH) on the Line of Heart point to an unhealthy heart, or a flirtatious tendency. It should be remembered that the Line of

Heart indicates the physical and medical aspects as well as the emotional and the psychological sides of the subject.

You will have to examine the effects of not only the islands, but also of other marks and their characteristics which leave their marked influence on the physical or emotional plane of the subject. Age is also a determining factor. In adolescence or in youth, there are good chances of the subject being involved in love affairs, while in old age the probabilities are that the defects will relate more to physical infirmities.

Dots on the Line: (Fig. 30-HH) These also indicate heart trouble; the trouble may, however, be emotional rather than physical. But if there are several deep and big dots, particularly on that portion of the Line of Heart under the Mount of Apollo, they are a sign of physical heart problems. White dots are messengers of success in love, but coloured dots are evil. Deep red dots show danger of apoplexy.

Breaks in the Line of Heart: Sometimes there is a break in the Line of Heart (Fig. 32-HH). This is a very serious defect, particularly, if found on both the hands at the same stage. It may indicate death. But if the two broken parts overlap, or a repair line covers the broken space, or the broken space is within a square (Fig. 35-HH), the subject will recover. To assess the seriousness of the effect of the break, the subsequent stage of the line must be examined. If the line at the subsequent stage is strong and healthy (Fig. 32-HH), chances of recovery are greater. It is also crucial to examine the direction of the line after the break. If it proceeds to any of the Mounts of Jupiter, Saturn, Apollo, or Mercury, it may indicate the disease pertaining to the mount.

If a broken line goes to any of the mounts and becomes deeper and reddish, it is the harbinger of impending health trouble. But if, instead of proceeding towards any of the mounts, an off-shoot of the line (before the break) moves in that direction, it may signify attraction to the type of person represented by that mount.

If many short breaks are observed on the line, it alludes to improper functioning of the heart, or disappointments in many love affairs (Fig. 61-HH). If the end of the broken line turns downwards and cuts the Line of Head, it indicates either mental shock due to failure, or break in a love affair, or thrombosis of the brain due to failure of the heart. If there is a star on the Line of Head where the broken line of heart cuts it, it is still worse.

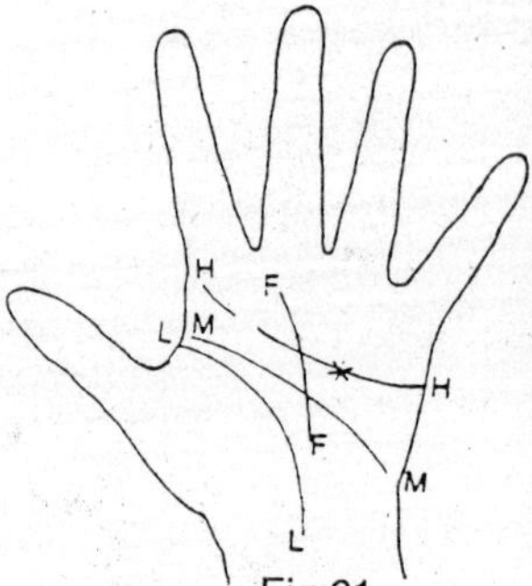

Fig 61

If there is a cross or cross-bar, or a dot, or some such negative sign (Fig. 40-HH) at the point of the break, it indicates that the subject's chances of recovery are bleak.

A Star on the Line of Heart: If the star (Fig. 61-HH) is a small one, the native may survive after a heart attack at the age indicated by this mark (age to be reckoned on the Line of Heart). But if the star is big, it indicates death.

Fork at the End: If the Line of Heart splits into two towards the end, and one long prong goes to the Mount of Luna and ends there in a star, then the indication is madness inherited through genes.

A Circle: The mark of a small circle (Fig. 36-HH) or any other harmful mark on the Line of Heart under the Mount of Apollo denotes loss of vision.

A Square: A square on the Line of Heart shows the ability to preserve or safeguard oneself against external influences.

NOTE: Any bad mark on the Line of Heart at the point it is cut by the Line of Fate shows financial troubles arising out of love affairs.

To estimate age on the Line of Heart, see Fig. 39.

11

Major Lines of the Hand
The Line of Fate

The Line of Fate is the fourth major line. It is also called the Line of Wealth. Some palmists also call it the Line of Saturn because it proceeds in the direction of that mount; and in hands where this line is complete, it generally ends on the Mount of Saturn (Fig. 62).

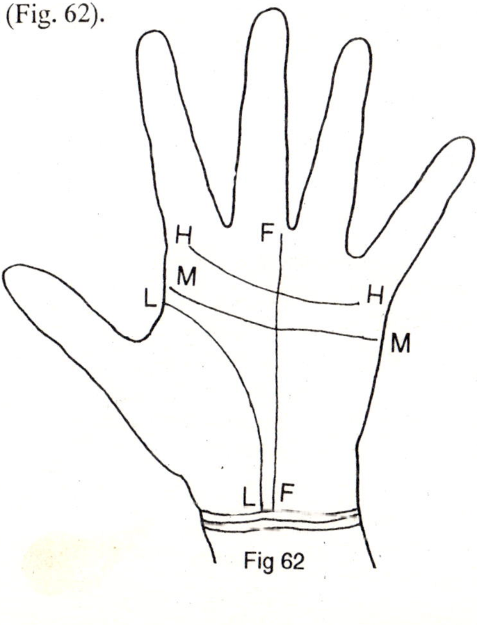

Fig 62

Characteristics

It goes without saying that no single line in the hand should be examined and assessed in isolation from others. A man who makes a mark in his life achieves it with a combination of intelligence and industry. He may have certain ambitions, and it is only by pursuing the right path and persevering in his efforts that he will be able to earn wealth. A tremendous zeal combined with pragmatism is essential to obtain the right perspective in the achievement of his goal. Therefore, even a long Line of Fate in a philosophic, psychic, or conic hand does not, necessarily, bring in that amount of wealth which even a short line (Fig. 54-FF) in the square hand does. Why is that so ?

The subject with a square hand is more practical, and worldly success is his guiding passion, but a man with a conical hand is more interested in the field of art. For the philosophic type, the world is an illusion, and money—an impediment in the path of spiritual progress. The psychic hand pursues the 'psyche', and not worldly riches. Therefore it is necessary to look at the type of hand and read the Line of Fate accordingly. To earn wealth, one has to work, and not indulge in day-dreaming.

According to palmistry, it is desirable that a complete Line of Fate should terminate at the Mount of Saturn. When this line is strong and deep, and goes on to the Mount of Saturn, it indicates (unless the Mount of Saturn has evil marks, or the Saturn finger is defective) all the good qualities of Saturn such as deep-thinking, far-sightedness, wisdom, and sobriety. These traits in any person are his assets which will help him to make money. If the line is faint, indistinct, or absent in the earlier part (the commencement of the line is taken from the wrist, and the termination, at the Mount of Saturn), but deep and well-cut on the Mount of Saturn, it indicates success in old age.

The Line of Fate should be deep and well-cut to bestow a positive influence on the subject. If it is not so deep and well-cut as the other major lines—the Lines of Life, Head, and Heart—then the success gained will not be in as great a measure as a deep, clear-cut line should bestow.

The question of colour has no significance in the Line of

Fate. Unlike the colours of the Lines of Life, Head, and Heart which affect the health of the subject, colour does not play such an important role in the case of the Line of Fate. Ancient palmists have stated that if the line is of a deep red colour, and goes straight to the third phalange of the finger of Saturn, it indicates an ignoble death.

To revert to a deep and clear-cut line: if this character continues from the commencement to its termination point at the Mount of Saturn, the subject enjoys good fortune throughout his life; but if, at places, it is faint and indistinct, or shallow, it indicates difficulties during that period of life (age to be reckoned on the Line of Fate). For example, if the line is deep and clear-cut in its initial stages (Fig. 63-FF), the subject will enjoy good luck during the early period of life. If it is so during the middle portion, the subject will be well off during the middle part of the life; and if the line is deep and clear-cut only on the Mount of Saturn, there will be success and affluence during old age.

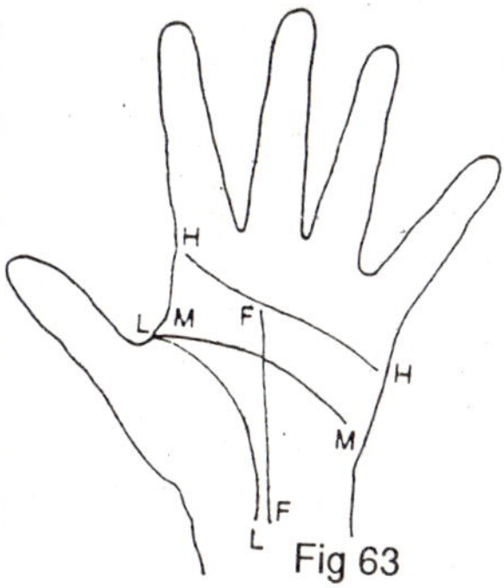

Fig 63

Course of the Line

Commencement: There are certain usual points from where the Line of Fate commences. These points have a significance of their own.

When the Line of Fate commences from the base of the palm—between the termination of the Line of Life and the Mount of Luna—and is well-defined and straight while going up to the Mount of Saturn (Fig. 62-FF), it indicates that the subject will be able to build up a good fortune through his own efforts and with the assistance of family members.

If the Line of Fate does not commence from the base of the palm and instead, i) begins from the centre of the palm, between the base of the palm and the Line of Head (Fig. 64A-FF), or ii) from the Line of Head onwards (Fig. 64B-FF), or iii) from the

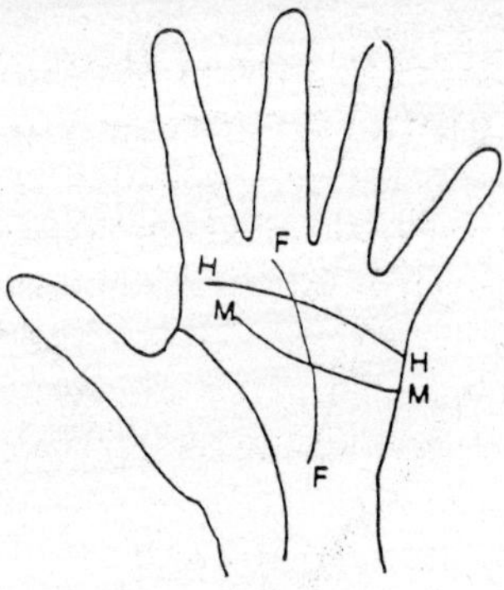

Fig 64 A

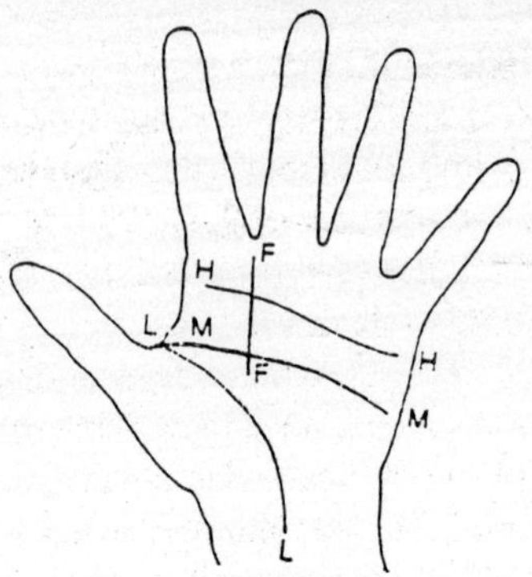

Fig 64 B

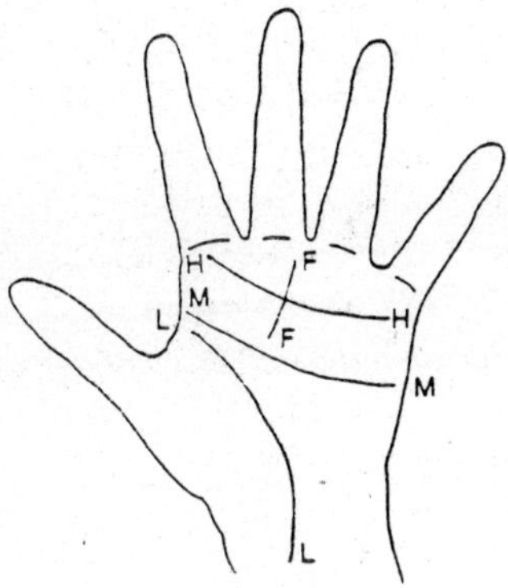

Fig 64 C

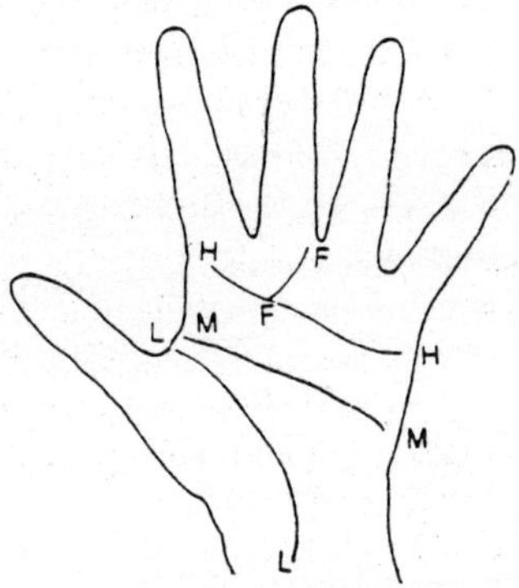

Fig 64 D

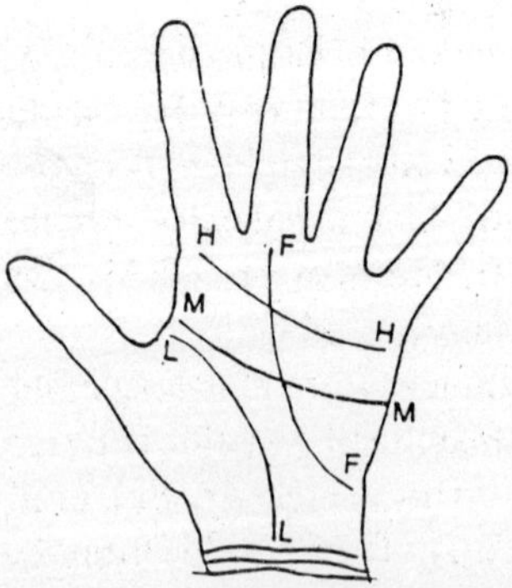

Fig 65

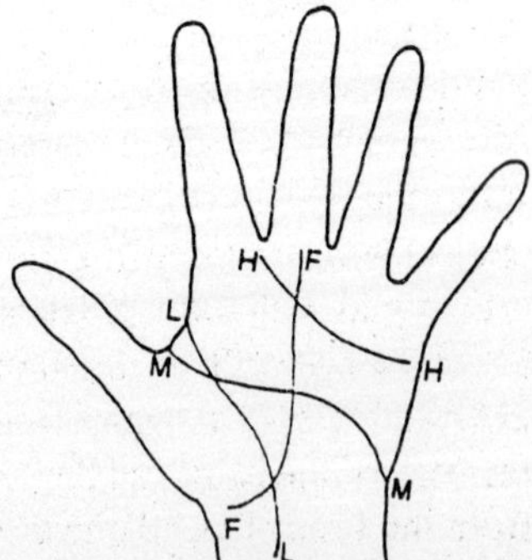

Fig 66

Quadrangle (Fig. 64C-FF), or iv) from the Line of Heart onwards (Fig. 64D-FF), it denotes success late in life.

NOTE: While reckoning age on the Line of Fate, the portion towards the base of the palm is taken as the early part of life, and the portion towards the Mount of Saturn as the latter part of life.

When the Line of Fate commences on the Mount of Luna, cuts across the Line of Life and goes to the centre of the palm, proceeds towards the Mount of Saturn and ends there (Fig. 65-FF), the subject achieves success in life. He also receives the help or patronage of friends, relatives, or other influential parties. At times the assistance may be in the form of good advice, useful introductions, or recommendations to other parties. In many hands, it has been verified that the help or patronage extended came from members of the opposite sex.

When the Line of Fate commences from the Mount of Venus, cuts the Line of Life and proceeds to the Mount of Saturn (Fig. 66-FF), it also indicates good fortune, but with the assistance of relatives. At times, family members chalk out the subject's career.

These are the usual commencing points. Besides these there are cases when the commencing point is unusual.

Readers are reminded that there are generally three bracelets at the place where the palm is joined to the forearm (Fig. 67). That which is nearest the palm is called the first bracelet; lower down is the second bracelet and the one nearest the arm is called the third bracelet.

When the Line of Fate commences from the first bracelet, it indicates that the native will have to shoulder family responsibilities at an early or premature age.

If the line commences from the third bracelet, it indicates some bereavement or intense grief in the early part of life.

If the Line of Fate commences from any of the bracelets and reaches

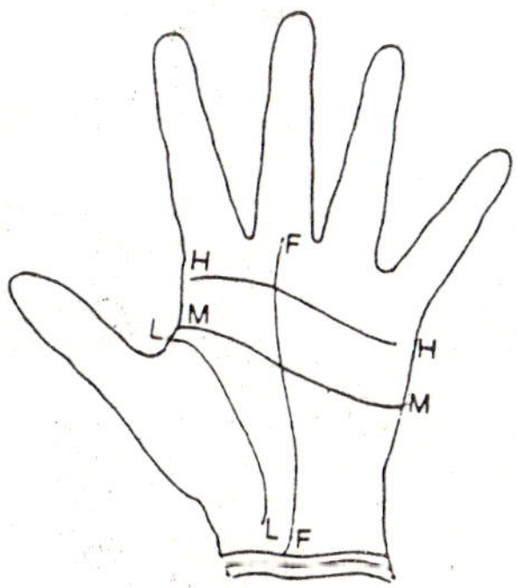

Fig 67

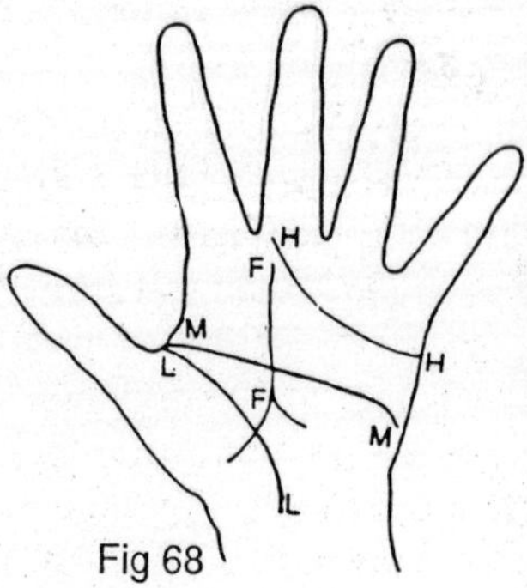

Fig 68

the third phalange of the Saturn finger (Fig. 67-FF), it shows an unusual destiny. If the other indications in the hand are good, this unusual destiny may indicate a good career, but if the other lines are not good, it points to failure in the career.

Commencing with a fork (Fig. 68-FF) alludes to adoption of the subject by a relation, specially when one fork reaches the Mount of Venus. Sometimes it also represents a divorce taking place between the subject's mother and father, a consequent court case, with each party claiming the child.

If the Line of Fate is broken at the point where the two prongs of the fork join it, and one prong goes well up to the Mount of Luna (Fig. 69-FF), then there is a danger of drowning, or of being a victim of intrigue made by the subject's beloved.

The line commencing from a star at the base of the hand (Fig. 70-FF) connotes financial misfortune to parents at the early stage of the subject's life. If, in addition, there is a star on the Mount of Venus, there could also be a death in the family, or early death of one of the parents, and consequent financial disaster.

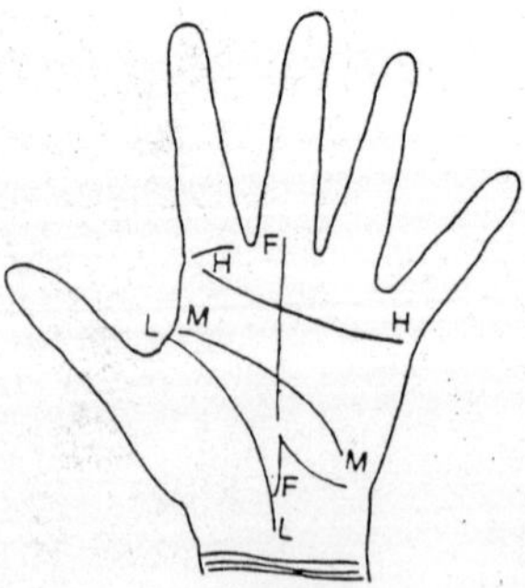

Fig 69

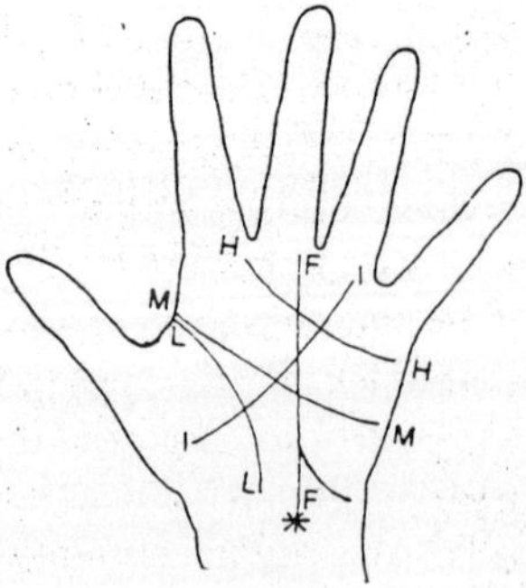

Fig 70

Curvature: As the Line of Fate traverses across the palm, it is subject to numerous influences.

Lines Merging with the Line of Fate: All lines merging with the Line of Fate make it deeper and stronger, and help the subject in the furtherance of his career. If the line is thin and indistinct at the commencement, or is chained or weak otherwise, and a line merging with it makes it stronger, it should be interpreted as outside influence affecting the native's life positively, and helping him to rise in his career.

In the case of many ladies, it has been found that a line from the Mount of Luna merges with the Line of Fate (Fig. 70- FF), making it stronger. It was also confirmed that, at the stage when the line from the Mount of Luna merged with the Line of Fate (age to be reckoned on the Line of Fate), the women married into very rich families.

If a line coming from the Mount of Venus merges with the Line of Fate, close relations will be of immense help to the subject.

The strength of the merging line and to what extent it is beneficial to the subject can be gauged from the condition of the Line of Fate after the merger. If it improves only slightly, the impact of the influence is good but not substantial. But if after the merger the line shows a marked improvement, the beneficial impact is substantial.

A Double Line: A double line is very fortunate (Fig. 71-FF FF) because it lends strong support to the main line, and makes up for any break or indistinctness at any place of the main line. If the double line starts from one of the prongs of the fork at the commencement of the main line and goes to the Mount of Apollo, it confers honour and wealth on the subject, giving him a brilliant career.

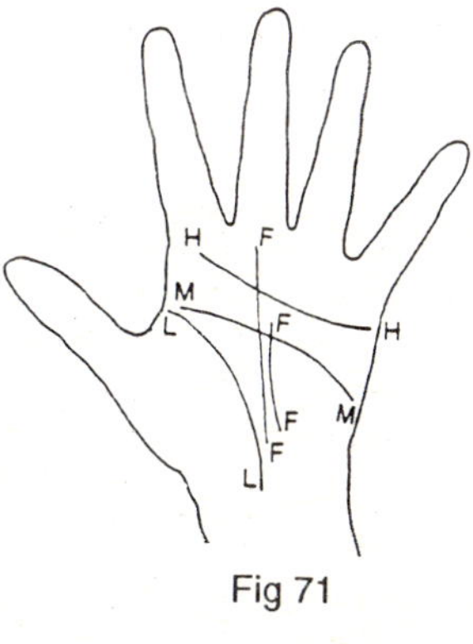

Fig 71

Termination: If the Line of Fate runs its usual course up to

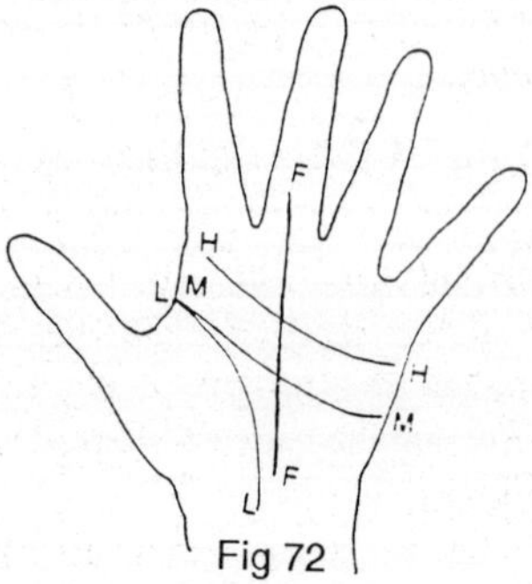

Fig 72

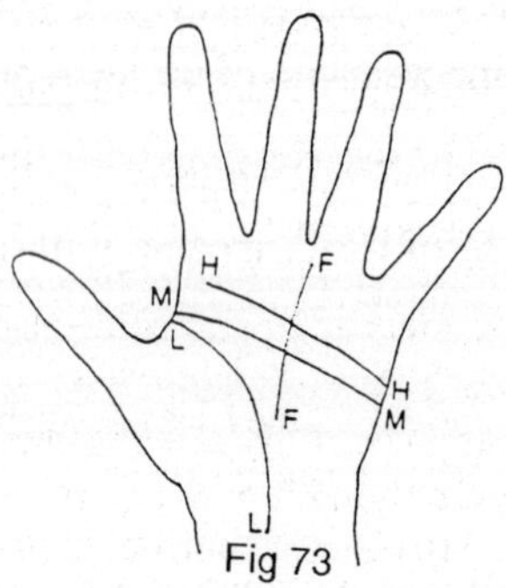

Fig 73

the centre of the palm, and then goes on to the Mount of Jupiter and ends there, the subject will have high ambitions, particularly, in the political or religious sphere, and these will be fulfilled. If the Line of Fate, instead of commencing from the base of the hand, emanates from the Mount of Luna, the ambitions of the subject will be fulfilled due to the patronage of some other party, probably of the opposite sex. At times it also indicates a good marriage which brings about rise in fortune.

If the Line of Fate ends in the third phalange of the Saturn finger (Fig. 72-FF), the subject will die an ignoble death or face imprisonment.

If it terminates in the Mount of Saturn, the native will earn well even in old age.

If a good Line of Fate ends in the Mount of Apollo (Fig. 73-FF), it indicates success in arts, authorship, etc.

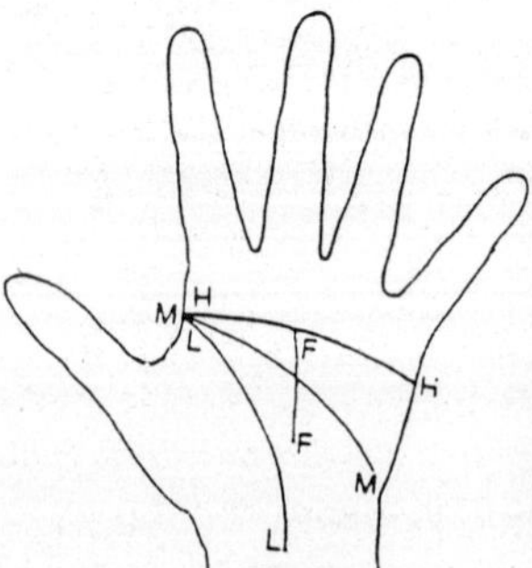

Fig 74

A good Line of Fate ending in the Mount of Mercury denotes success in business or commerce. Care should be taken not to confuse this line with the Line of Mercury (also called the Line of Health), which starts from the base of the palm or from the Line of Life, and goes to the Mount of Mercury.

If the Line of Fate terminates at the Line of Heart (Fig. 74-FF), there is a cessation of income due to some weakness of the heart or love affair.

If the Line of Fate ends in the Line of Head, income will cease; the cessation of income will be due to an error of judgement.

NOTE: If the Line of Fate breaks at the Line of Heart or Head and then continues again, it should be treated as indicating a break in one's career due to problems of heart or head, according to the place of the break, and thereafter, the recontinuation of career.

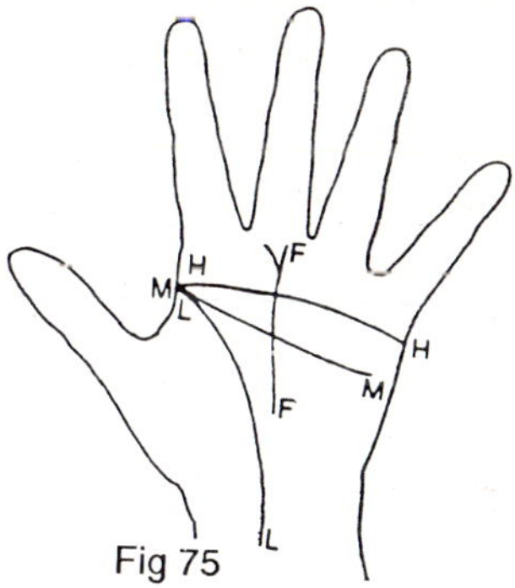

Fig 75

A Line of Fate terminating in a fork (Fig. 75-FF) or trident alludes to income from various sources according to the mounts to which the prongs go. If the prongs are feeble (not deep and well-cut), the income will not be high. But if the prongs are deep, clear-cut, and long, income derived from various sources will be good.

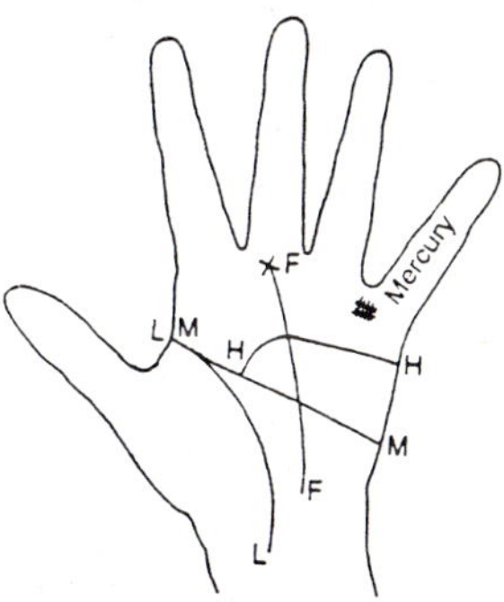

Fig 76

A Line of Fate ending in a tassel points towards a meagre income. It indicates waning of earning power.

If the line ends in a cross on the Mount of Saturn and there is a grille on the Mount of Mercury (Fig. 76-FF), the subject may face a violent death.

If the Line of Fate ends in a star on the Mount of Saturn, paralysis may strike the individual.

Absence of the Line

The absence of the Line of Fate has been interpreted by a school of palmists as absence of markedly good luck. But I hold a different view. After examining many hands in which the shape of the hand, the phalanges of the thumb, the fingers, mounts, the Lines of Head, Heart, and Life were well-balanced and without any serious flaws, and the Line of Fate was absent or very poorly marked, I found that owners of such hands had earned wealth, and also made a mark in their career. So, whenever we examine an otherwise good hand, with the Line of Fate being absent, it can be concluded that the subjects have risen by dint of their personal efforts. Such people are industrious and self-made.

Also, if the Line of Fate is absent, wholly or in part, and if the Line of Apollo is present at the stage where the Line of Fate is absent, it should be taken as repairing the absence of the Line of Fate. In fact, it acts as a sister line to the Line of Fate.

Defects

Whenever there is any defect on the Line of Fate, there will be difficulties or recession in good luck at the age where the defect is found. If there are defects in the early part of the line, and they correspond with defects in the same part of the Line of Life, the subject could suffer from ill health at that age. However, if the Line of Head is defective during that portion, it shows an undeveloped mind, lack of good education, or brain trouble. In case the Line of Heart is defective during its early portion, there may be a weak heart, or if the Mount of Venus is also over developed, the subject will be extra sensuous and too amorous to devote himself to the constructive side of life and build the foundations of a stable career. At times, a defect on the early portion of the Line of Life may also indicate indigent circumstances of the parents, or death of one of the parents due to which the subject may not do well. If the portion of the line beyond the defect is good, the native will ultimately overcome his difficulties. But if it is not so good, the problems created in the early part of life will be the beginning of continuing impediments, though not so serious.

If the Line of Fate is defective in the early part, and if a Line of Influence commencing from the Mount of Venus ends in a star on the Line of Fate, it indicates unfavourable circumstances due to the death of one of the parents. If, in addition, a line runs from the star and ends in an island on the Line of Head, it shows that the native has received such a terrible shock due to the bereavement that he will not be able to make any progress in the early part of life.

If the Line of Fate is uneven, that is, it is not deep and clear-cut throughout its course—it indicates that the periods represented by the deep and clear-cut portion of it will be periods of success and inflow of money, while the periods where it is thin and shallow will be periods of difficulties or less earning.

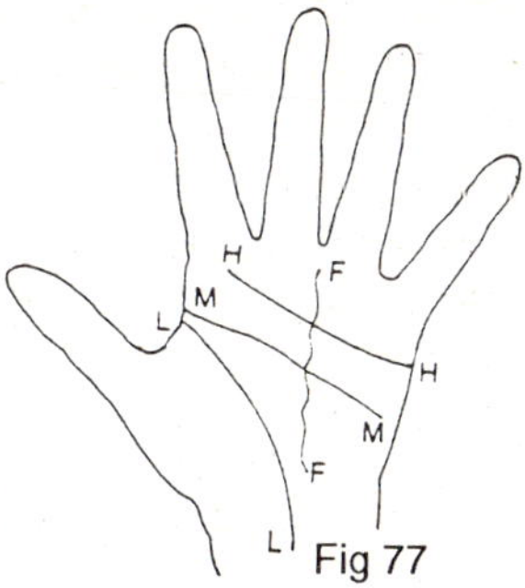

Fig 77

Since the Line of Fate indicates a career, if the line is wavy (Fig. 77-FF), the subject will not stick to one profession or occupation; he will continue to change his career constantly. Inability to follow one course steadfastly will make him unsuccessful. If, in addition to being wavy, the line has breaks or small cross-bars cutting it, there will be many impediments.

Off-shoots (thin and fine lines) branching out from the Line of Fate can be divided into two categories. Those which emanate from the Line of Fate and proceed downwards (Fig. 78-FF) towards the wrist show that life will be harder and the native will have to overcome many impediments and difficulties. But hair lines proceeding upwards (Fig. 79-FF) towards the mounts increase hope and ambition, and fulfillment thereof.

It will help the readers to keep in mind the general principle that all upward off-shoots or branches or hair lines are good, and that those moving downwards are evil.

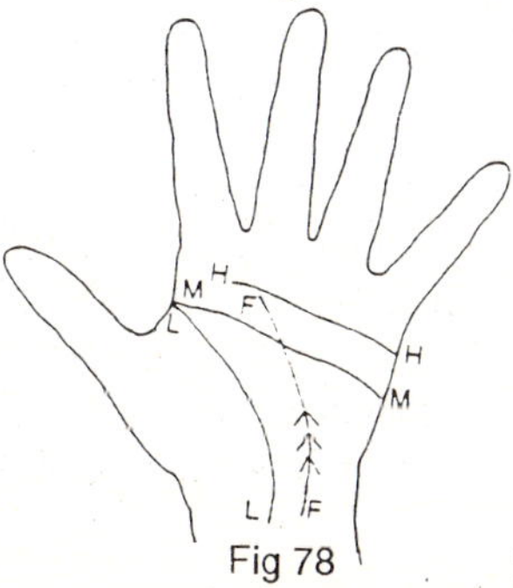

Fig 78

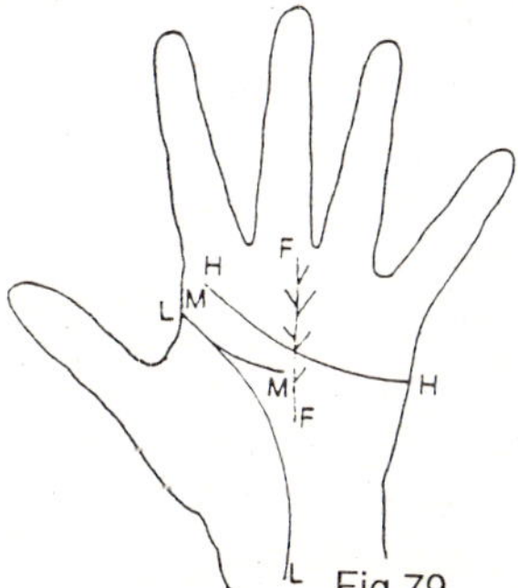

Fig 79

On examining the Line of Life corresponding to the age on the Line of Fate, where off-shoots appear on the latter, you will observe that, in many hands, there is a correlation between the off-shoots and the health of the subject. When the Line of Life indicates ill health—hope, ambition, and encouragement are dimmed (downward hair lines denoting the same). But when the Line of Life shows vigour and vitality, the Line of Fate shows upward off-shoots.

If there is an island on the Line of Head corresponding to the period of downward off-shoots on the Line of Fate, it indicates a waning of luck due to brain brouble. If, however, the island is not on the Line of Head but on the Line of Heart, the waning of fortune would be due to a weak heart or love affair.

Even when upward off-shoots start form the Line of Fate, it has to be observed if they are being cut by any Lines of Influence commencing from the Mount of Venus. If such lines cut the upward off-shoots, the cutting would create hurdles in the path of progress, but the native would still progress despite these impediments. These lines act as hurdles but not as stoppages.

In many hands, thin oblique lines cross the Line of Fate. They may commence from the Mount of Venus or the Mount of Luna, or may be other chance lines. They may be either lines of influence or worry lines. Worry lines are generally found in the hands of subjects who have a nervous temperament.

In principle, all lines cutting the Line of Fate are considered impediments (Lines of Influence have been dealt with in another chapter and we shall not expand them here). It would suffice to say that all lines which start from below and merge with the Line of Fate, making it stronger after the merger, are good and favourable, while those which cut it are impediments and obstructions.

There can be so many commencing points for these lines. For example, if the cutting line starts from the Line of Life and cuts the Line of Fate, the subject's health may be affected adversely; if the cutting line commences from the Line of Head, it indicates mental illness or wrong judgement; if it starts from the Line of Heart, the source of trouble will be matters of the heart, which will interfere with the subject's career. Given below are some more specific examples:

- A line from a star on the Mount of Jupiter, and cutting the Line of Fate, points at vaulting ambition which overleaps itself.
- If a line from a star on the Mount of Jupiter cuts the Line of Fate, and if there is an island on the Line of Fate where the line cuts, there are indications of extravagance and consequent financial difficulties. The native will spend heavily in the mistaken belief that his extravagance will help him in the fulfilment of his ambitions.
- If the hand shows any dishonest tendencies (for example, a bad Mercurian hand, an overdeveloped Mount of Mercury with a grille, a large third phalange of the fourth finger, twisted little finger, etc.), and a line starting from a grille on the Mount of Mercury cuts the Line of Fate, the native's career will suffer due to his own dishonesty.
- If a Line of Influence from the Mount of Venus ends in a star, and a line from such a Line of Influence cuts the Line of Fate, a close relation may die, obstructing the career of the subject.

These are examples of how we have to ascertain the cause which will be responsible for an adverse fate. The condition of the Line of Fate after the cut is very important; for if it subsequently becomes thin and feeble, the impact of misfortune will be great. But if the line is broken after the cut, it implies a complete break in career. If such a cutting line approaches the Line of Fate but does not actually cut it, it should be viewed as an apprehension or a probable cut. For since lines change in the future, it may turn into a cutting line at a later stage.

Marks on the Line

An Island: An island on the Line of Fate (Fig. 80-FF) indicates a difficult financial period. Care should be taken to distinguish an island from an off-shoot of the Line of Fate. When the Line of Fate splits into two, and the two ends meet again, forming a line and proceeding further in the course, the island is a harmful feature. If the line splits into two, and one line continues, and the other line does not join the main line but runs as an independent line (no space being completely enclosed by the split lines), then it is not an island, but a mere off-shoot which is considered good; it adds fillip to fortune if the main line appears to be as good after the off-shoot as it was before it.

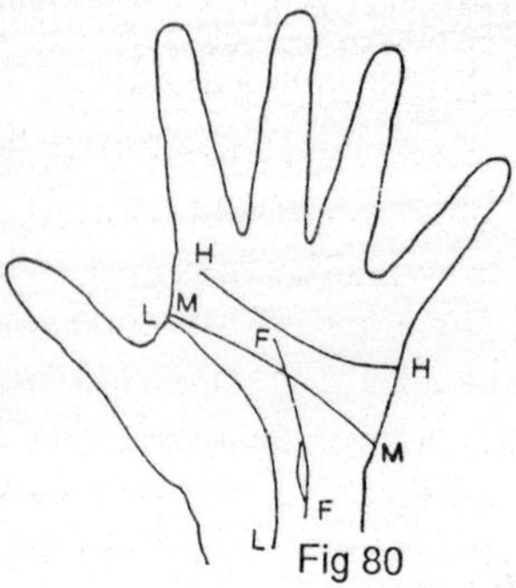

Fig 80

In many female hands, an island on the Line of Fate also implies a clandestine love affair which impedes progress. For confirmation of this, observe if there is a Line of Influence coming from the Mount of Venus and ending in this island on the Line of Fate, or if there is an island on the Line of Heart at the corresponding age.

A Cross-bar: Cross-bars cutting the Line of Fate indicate obstructions in earning. Each horizontal line cutting the Line of Fate is an obstruction. The severity of the obstructions is determined from the depth of these cutting lines. If after the cut, the Line of Fate becomes indistinct or shows a break, the obstruction should be regarded as serious. But if the bar (horizontal cutting line) is weak, faint, and small, and the quality (depth and clarity) of the Line of Fate does not suffer, the impediment should be considered as relatively mild.

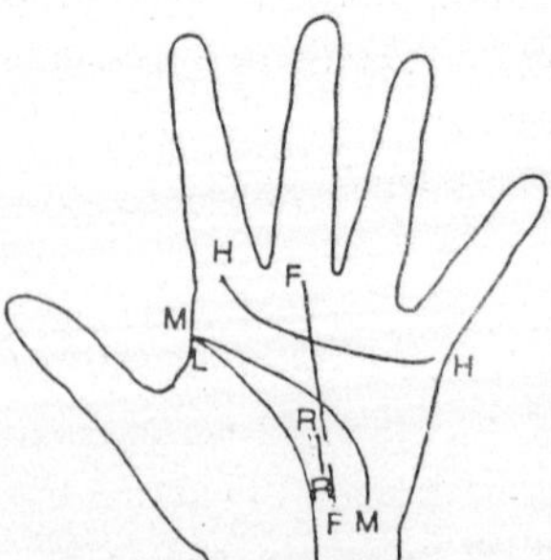

Fig 81

A Break: A break in the Line of Fate is a serious defect (Fig. 81-FF). It indicates a break in the career or discontinuity in earning during the period the break continues. In such cases one must note the trend of the Line of Fate after the break. If it continues in the same direction again and is of the same quality, the native's earning capacity or career will resume as before. But if the line after the break is weak, the native will not be able to earn as much as he was earning prior to the break.

When after a break, the new line moves in a different direction or towards a different mount, there will be a complete change in the subject's career; if the new line is stronger than the older one, it denotes greater prosperity for the native.

We have stated above that a break in the Line of Fate is one of the major defects. It can be removed if:

- the two broken lines overlap each other;
- there is a repair line parallel to the main line, covering the distance of the break in the main line (Fig. 81-RR); or
- the broken space is enclosed by a square. In such a case, the break in the Line of Fate will not have harmful consequences.

A Cross: A cross on the Line of Fate resulting in a break in the latter (Fig. 82-FF), alludes to reversal in fortune. A cross near the Line of Fate without a break will have an adverse effect on one of the subject's relations.

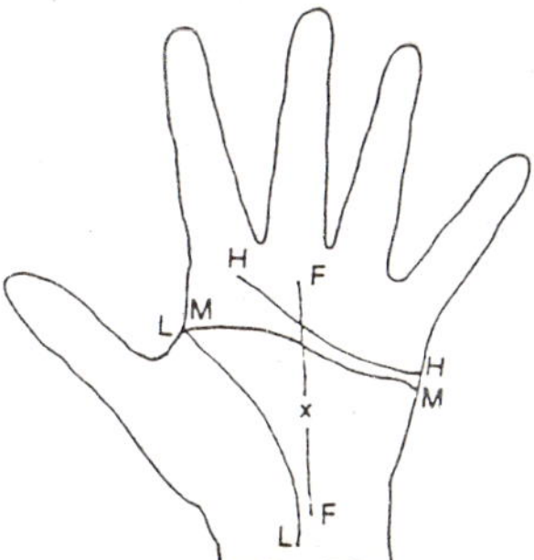

Fig 82

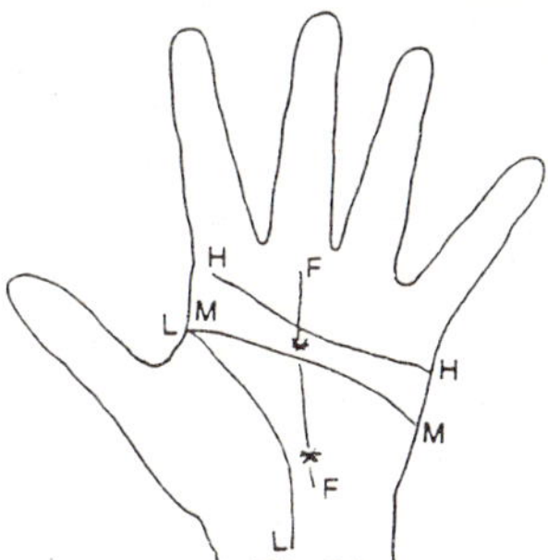

Fig 83

A Star: A star on the line (Fig. 83-FF) signifies financial disaster at the age indicated by the star (age to be reckoned on the Line of Fate).

NOTE: A cross and a star on the Line of Fate indicate serious obstacles to fortune at that age.

Estimating Age

In years gone by, palmists laid down some rules to determine age on the Line of Fate but their systems of reckoning age on the line differed widely. Therefore, given below are a set of rules, the validity of which has been confirmed by experience.

The Line of Fate originates from the base of the hand, either from the Line of Life, or from the inner side of the Line of Life; or from the space between the Line of Life and the Mount of Luna; or from the Mount of Luna itself. The beginning of the Line of Fate should be interpreted as the early years of life.

The point at which the Line of Fate touches the Line of Head, should be taken as thirty-five years of age. If the Line of Head is lower than the normal position, the age where the Line of Fate touches the Line of Head should be taken as thirty.

The stage where the Line of Fate touches or crosses the Line of Heart is taken as fifty years. But if the Line of Heart is higher than its normal position, the age at the crossing point of the Line of Heart and the Line of Fate is taken as fifty-six, and the portion beyond the Line of Heart (i.e., proceeding on to the mounts) as an age beyond fifty-six years.

It is very difficult to specify the exact age on each hand because some people live well upto ninety years of age or more. Also, the shape of each hand differs. Then again, the position of the Line of Heart in all hands is not in the same place. While examining the lines on the subject's hand, the age should be identified with the aid of some mark, cut, or break, and then that should be tallied with the information the subject gives with regard to certain past occurences. Future timings can be reckoned accordingly.

12

Minor Lines of the Hand
The Line of Apollo

Apart from the Lines of Life, Head, Heart, and Fate which constitute the Major Lines of the hand, there are certain Minor Lines which have their own significance.

Apollo means Sun, and hence, some palmists also call this as the Line of the Sun. Although its starting points vary on different hands, since it terminates at the Mount of Apollo, it is known by that name.

The Line of Apollo represents wealth, honour, learning, and artistic or intellectual attainments. Many palmists call it the second Line of Fate, but it would be more appropriate to call it a sister line to the Line of Fate: firstly, because it is generally parallel to the Line of Fate, and makes up for the latter's deficiencies, and secondly, because it also signifies wealth. We may illustrate this by stating that even in the absence of a Line of Fate, the subject will be wealthy if the Line of Apollo is present.

Besides wealth, the line also stands for honour and reputation. In Hindu texts it is called *Vidya Rekha* or the Line of Learning and since the finger of Apollo is associated with art, this line also stands for arts and artistic appreciation. Other features such as the shape of the hand, the tips of the fingers, the mounts, and the

Lines of Head and Fate should be taken into consideration to determine the extent of good influence that a positive Line of Apollo would exert. Thus, a native may occupy a high rank and status, or may be wealthy; he may reach intellectual heights, yet may not be an artist.

The Line of Apollo is not found in all hands. In many hands, the line is only found on the Mount of Apollo, and is absent in the lower part of the hand. This is indicative of rank or honour or wealth in the latter part of life. It has been observed that a long Line of Apollo straight from the base of the palm right up to the Mount of Apollo exists only in a few hands, and such persons achieve fame in their own spheres.

Characteristics

The Line of Apollo is deemed good if it is long, deep, and well-cut. If well formed in both hands, the Line of Apollo is a guarantee for success in life. If it is very deep and if the hand is conic, it is likely that the native will overexert himself and may suffer ill health. A pinkish or red line indicates pursuit of an artistic career, but if the line is pale, the subject will lack in energy and application despite his artistic aptitude. If the line is broad or wavy, the subject will be wanting in concentration and perseverance. A chained or ill-formed line hinders success.

Course of the Line

Commencement: A long Line of Apollo without any flaws is a good one. If it starts at a point between the Mount of Luna and Venus, or at the Mount of Luna and goes right up to and on the Mount of Apollo, it is considered to be long.

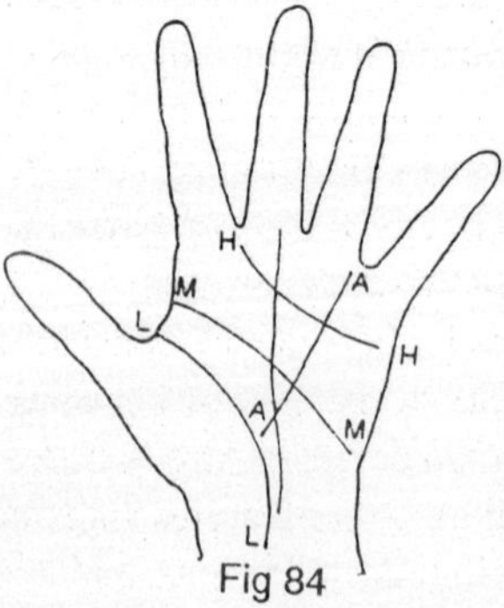

Fig 84

If the Line of Apollo starts from the Line of Life (Fig. 84-AA) or from inside the Mount of Venus, family members or relations will help the subject to achieve success.

If the line starts from the Mount of Luna (Fig. 85-AA), the subject

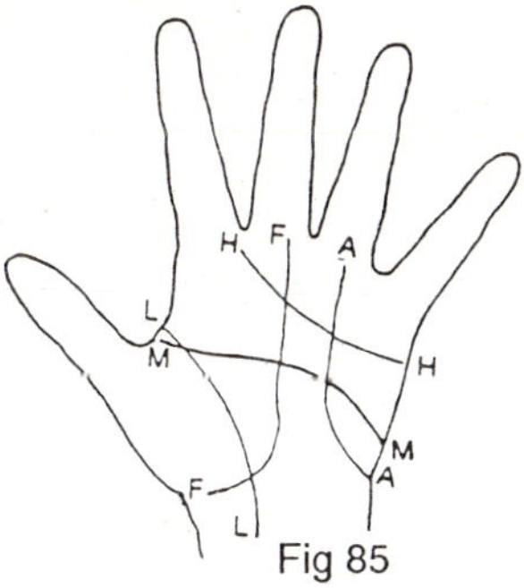

Fig 85

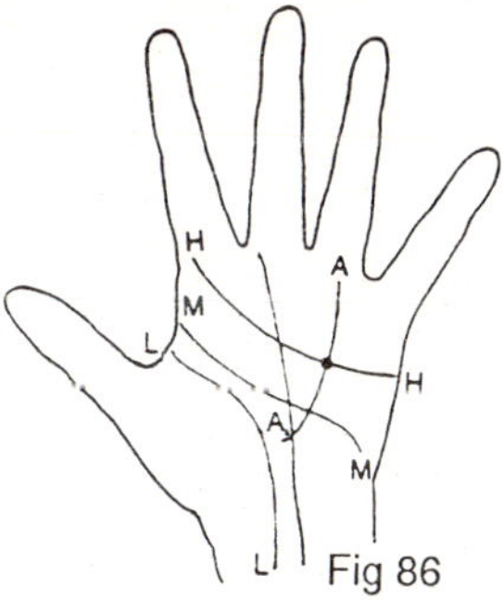

Fig 86

will taste the fruits of success due to help and patronage of others, probably from a member of the opposite sex.

If, in addition, the Line of Head is sloping and going towards the Mount of Luna, the subject is endowed with a good imagination, and will find fulfillment and success in the field of art, poetry, drama, music, and painting.

Starting higher up from the Triangle (space between the Lines of Head and Life) (Fig. 86-AA), success will come to the subject only after middle age.

If the Line of Apollo commences from the Line of Heart (Fig. 87-AA), the subject will have to wait till old age to be successful. However, those pursuing an artistic career may derive inspiration from emotional relationships.

Commencing from the Upper Mount of Mars and going to the Mount of Apollo, the Line of Apollo signifies that the subject will put in substantial effort, face up to competition, and ultimately, achieve success (Fig. 88-AA).

If the line starts from the Triangle and stops at the Line of Head, and again starts from the Line of Head, it indicates that the subject will not be able to execute his schemes due to interference from others.

The best position for the line is to start at the base of the hand and go straight to the Mount of Apollo. This denotes a brilliant career, name, fame, and wealth.

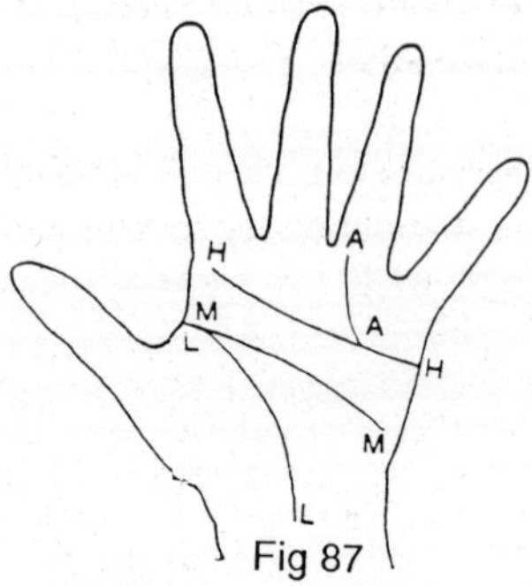

Fig 87

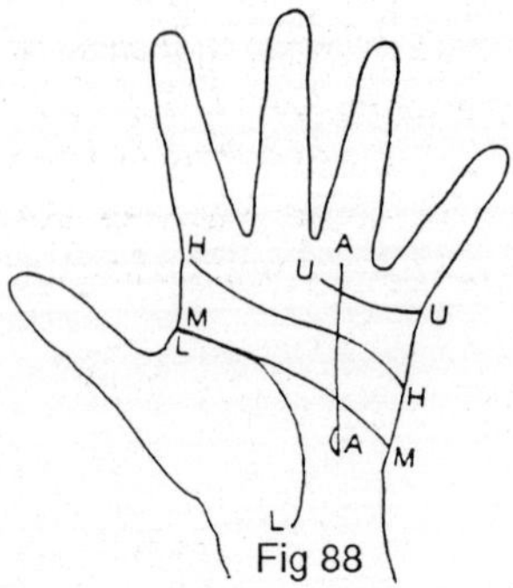

Fig 88

The Line of Apollo in Relation to Other Lines and Mounts: A good Line of Apollo can exert its positive influence only in collaboration with other good features in the hand.

Even if the Line of Apollo is good, it will not bestow its full or good effect if the Line of Fate is absent.

If the Line of Apollo is poorly formed, the Line of Health has an island on it, and the Line of Fate also suffers from serious defects, the native may become bankrupt.

If the line is good but the hand is hollow (that is, the Plain of Mars is very depressed), the line cannot exert a totally positive effect. If, in addition, the fingers are twisted, the subject will utilise his talents for harmful purposes such as swindling others; success will be fleeting and short-lived.

If the Line of Apollo is cut by a long Line of Union (or Line of Marriage as it is popularly called), a loss of position and honour due to a scandalous love affair or marriage is likely (Fig. 88-AA, UU).

An island at the beginning of the Line of Apollo (Fig. 88-AA) indicates a clandestine love affair which will help the native. If the island is not at the beginning but further on, and the line at the corresponding age is also defective, the subject may suffer from eye diseases. However, if the Line of Life is not defective, the subject may lose money or his reputation.

If the Mounts of Saturn and Luna are overdeveloped or too depressed, and have bad marks, and the Line of Head is sloping down on the Mount of Luna, and there is also a cross touching the Line of Apollo, there is a danger of mental imbalance. The situation is worse if, instead of one cross, there are two crosses touching the Line of Apollo.

If a Line of Influence from the Mount of Venus touches the Line of Apollo but does not cut it, then the native will be successful and will be helped by his relatives.

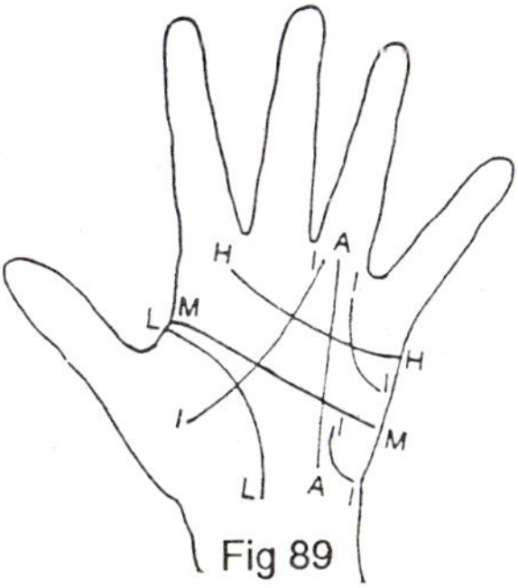

Fig 89

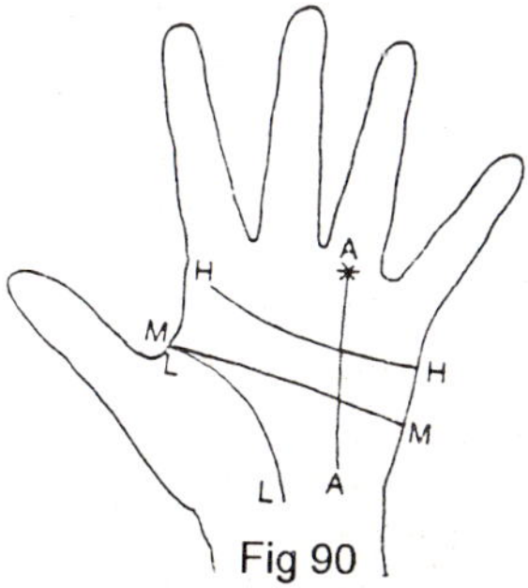

Fig 90

Lines of Influence from the Mounts of Venus and Luna which run upto a certain distance along the Line of Apollo (Fig. 89-I I) but do not touch it, indicate that the subject will receive a legacy.

If a good straight Line of Apollo reaches the Mount of Apollo, and if there is a star on that mount, the subject will enjoy extraordinary success in his career (Fig. 90).

A good Line of Apollo, accompanied by a good Line of Fate, and a well-developed Mount of Jupiter herald the crowning of ambition.

A good line and well-developed Mount of Jupiter denote honour and rank. The native will mingle in high society.

If the Lines of Apollo and Head are good, and the Apollo finger is also long and strong, the subject will be very wealthy. But if the

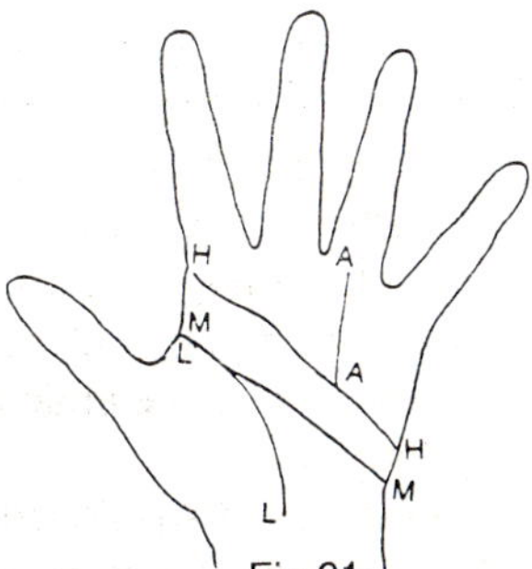

Fig 91

Line of Head is sloping and descends well into the Mount of

Luna (Fig. 91), and the third finger is almost as long as the second finger, the native may turn to be a gambler or a speculator.

A good Line of Apollo with well-developed Mounts of Mercury and Jupiter denotes riches. But if instead of the Mounts of Mercury and Jupiter, those of Luna and Venus are well-developed, the subject will devote his energies to the literary or artistic field and will acquire name and fame thereby. In this context readers are reminded that short nails develop the critical faculty. Without other good features, a person with short nails will criticise his friends and family members. But if he also has a good Line of Apollo and well-developed Mounts of Luna and Venus, the subject may become a good critic in the field of art or literature.

Termination: Certain interpretations based on the terminal points of the Line of Apollo are given below:

If the line terminates at a trident (Fig. 92-AA) (that is, forked with three prongs) on the Mount of Apollo, it indicates that the native will achieve name, fame, and wealth by his personal efforts; but if the fork has two prongs only, the native will divide his efforts in two directions, thereby depriving himself of any great success in either. The effect of the trident is felt in full measure when the prongs are wide apart, with all the three prongs being on the Mount of Apollo; or one prong going to the Mount of Saturn, the middle one going to the Mount of Apollo, and the third one proceeding to the Mount of Mercury. But if the trident is small and the prongs on the two sides are close to the middle one, then the level of success will be average.

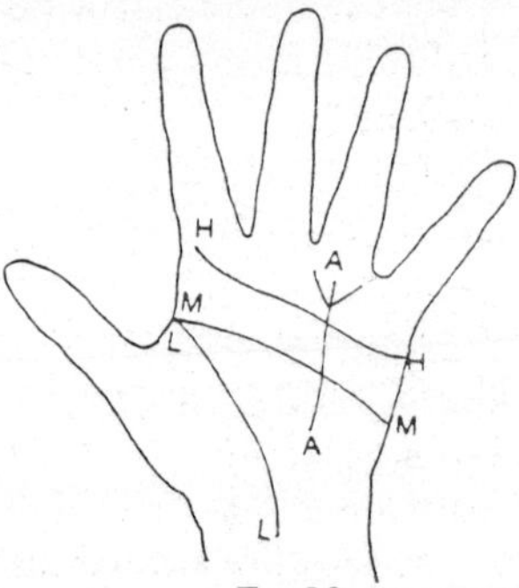

Fig 92

If the Line of Apollo terminates at the Mount of Mercury, the subject will give more weightage to the commercial side of art.

When the line ends on the Mount of Saturn, a tinge of morbidity will be added to the art.

When the Line of Apollo ends on the Mount of Apollo with several vertical lines running parallel to each other on the Mount (Fig. 93-AA), it indicates a frittering of energy in more than one direction. Hence, it will lead to failure due to divided attention. But if there are two small straight lines on either side of the Line of Apollo, the subject will achieve success and a good name; if these two lines are not straight but wavy, they allude to failure due to a dissipation of energy.

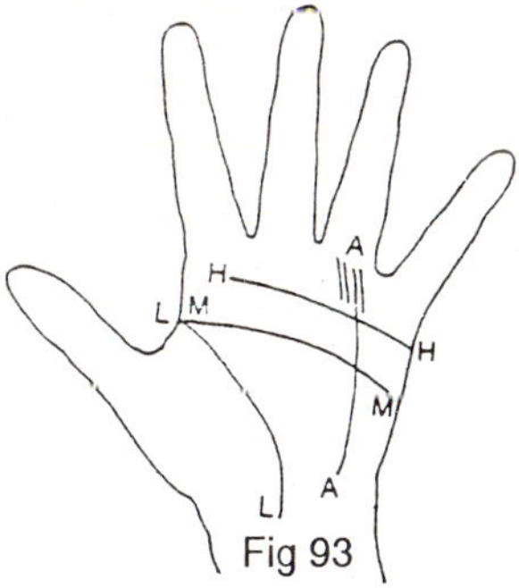

Fig 93

Defects

By now readers should be in a position to understand the features of the marks constituting defects. Some of these defects are further discussed below.

Off-shoots arising from the Line of Apollo are harmful if they go downwards. If the off-shoots are wavy, indistinct, or broken, or cut by cross-bars, they do not promote success, but bring about failure due to lack of continuity and perseverance on the part of the subject, even though they may proceed upwards.

Effects similar to those described above are produced if the Line of Apollo is broken at several places. If broken at one place only, it is not so serious, particularly, if the broken parts overlap each other, or there is a repair line, or the broken ends are enclosed by a square. If a Line of Influence from the Mount of Venus crosses the Line of Apollo at the point of the break, the failure may be attributed to a relative or friend who has an emotional involvement with the subject.

If the Line of Apollo is cut by a horizontal line from the Mount of Saturn, financial stringency will lead to failure. If cut by a horizontal line from Upper Mars, financial loss will be brought about by an enemy.

If the Line of Apollo is cut by a Line of Influence from the Mount of Venus (Fig. 94 AA, I I), the subject will lose money

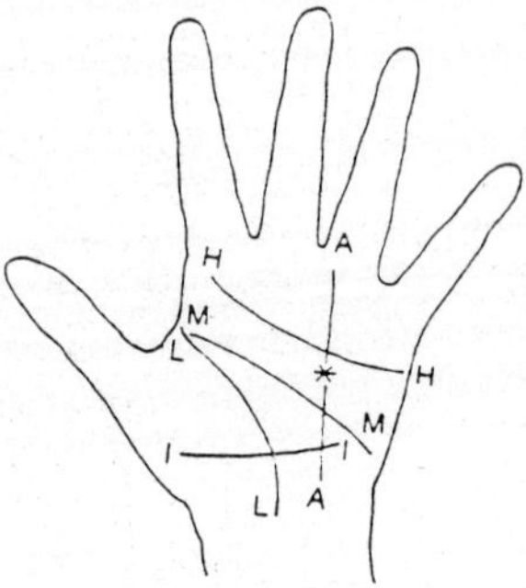

Fig 94

due to the influence of a relative or someone for whom he has affection.

If such a Line of Influence also cuts an upward off-shoot from the Line of Life, it is indicative of loss in a law suit. A distinction has to be made between the Line of Influence touching the Line of Apollo and the one cutting it. If it merely touches the Line of Apollo, the subject will win the law suit, but if it cuts the Line of Apollo, he will lose it.

Marks on the Line

Cross-bars: If the Line of Apollo is cut by numerous cross-bars, there will be impediments in the subject's career. Cuts on the early stages of the line (referring to the early part of life when the subject cannot have a career of his own) indicate misfortune to the parents.

A Star: A star on the Line of Apollo (Fig. 94-AA) signals a financial catastrophe or the ruining of the subject's reputation. If the condition of the line is good after this, the subject will recover from these problems.

A Spot or a Dot: Either of these two marks on the point where the Line of Apollo crosses the Line of Heart (Fig. 86-AA) could mean a loss of vision. If the dot is very deep, or the spot is black in colour, the subject is likely to be afflicted by blindness.

A Cross: A cross on the side of the percussion (and not on the side of the Line of Fate) which touches the Line of Apollo means that money will be hard to come by. Earning through artistic talents will also be meagre.

Estimating Age

Age on the Line of Apollo has to be reckoned as on the Line of Fate (Fig. 39)

13

Minor Lines of the Hand
The Line of Mercury or Health

This line is called the Line of Mercury, because if it runs its full course, it will generally end on the Mount of Mercury. It is also called the Line of Liver or Hepatica. This line represents the digestive powers, the functioning of the liver, and the secretion of bile. We are all aware of how our digestive powers affect our life, head and heart, clear thinking, and success. Any bad marks or defects on the Line of Health point to a defective digestion due to the improper functioning of the liver. Irritation, anger, confused thinking—all these are results of the poor secretion of the bile by the liver which is the largest gland in the human body.

The Line of Health is not found on all hands. In fact it is considered better if it is absent altogether, as its presence denotes ill health.

Characteristics

If the line is deep and well-marked, health will be good. If the Line of Life is not so good, then just as a good Line of Mars acts as a sister line to the Line of Life, and adds vitality to it—in the same manner—a good Line of Health makes up for any deficiencies on the Line of Life. Since many diseases of the mind and heart can be traced to defective digestion and imperfect secretion of the bile, wind trouble, etc., any defects on the Line of Head and Heart will be mollified to a certain extent if the Line of Health is good. Conversely, if the Line of Health is chained, islanded, broken, or ladder-like in appearance, it may adversely affect the mental health or even the proper functioning of the heart, as in the human body, one organ is dependent upon another.

If the Line of Health is long and good, and well-marked, it shows continued good health (the age is to be reckoned from the starting point at the base of the hand). The portion ending on the Mount of Mercury shows old age. If the line is good in some portions and not so good in others, the part of life represented by the good portion will be healthy, while that represented by a poor line, or a line having defects will signify periods of illness or chronic ill health. If the line is yellowish, it shows an imperfect functioning of the liver.

Course of the Line

Commencement: The Line of Health usually originates from the Line of Life (Fig. 95-NN); the space between the Lines of Life and Fate (Fig. 96-NN); from the Mount of Luna; or from the Plain of Mars.

If the Line of Health emanates from the Line of Life, it is deemed defective, while its commencement from other places is considered beneficial.

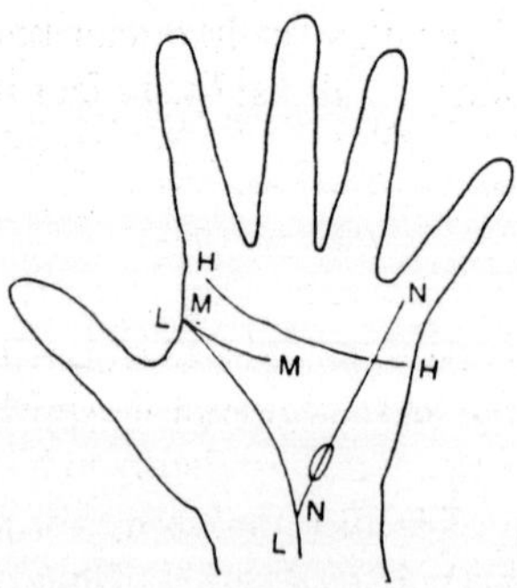

Fig 95

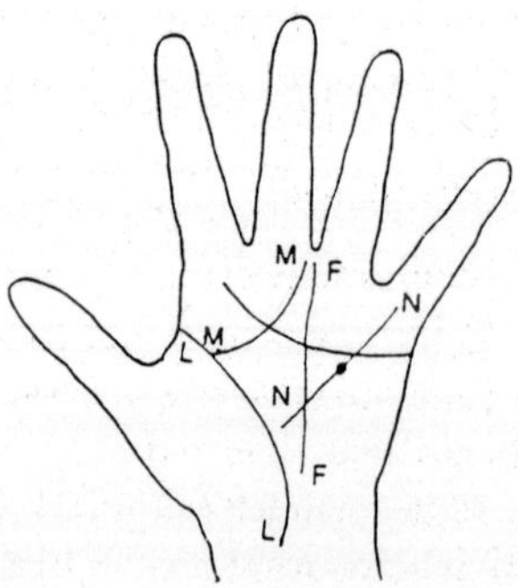

Fig 96

Off-shoots: If off-shoots rise from the Line of Health on the Mount of Mercury, they signify good health.

If the line is deep and well-marked, and an off-shoot goes down towards the base of the hand, it indicates that the subject needs to put in concentrated effort.

An off-shoot of the line going to the Mount of Jupiter indicates success in business due to good executive abilities. If, in addition, there is a star on the Mount of Jupiter, the subject will receive the patronage and help of influential people.

If an off-shoot of the line goes to the Mount of Saturn, the subject will achieve success due to hard work, sobriety, and far-sightedness.

An off-shoot going to the Mount of Apollo is indicative of shrewdness in business, and success.

While judging the sphere of success, the three phalanges of the finger must be examined. The first phalange represents intellectual attainments; the second denotes scientific or professional attainments; and the third alludes to commercial attainments.

An off-shoot of the Line of Health merging with the Line of Head points to success due to mental efforts.

Termination: The usual point of termination for the Line of Health is the Mount of Mercury.

If the line is cut by the Line of Union or Marriage at its termination (Fig. 97-NN, UU), it indicates that such a union will obstruct the career of the subject.

If the line is cut by a cross-bar on the Mount of Mercury, and the hand shows dishonest tendencies (such as crooked fingers), the subject's deceitful nature will hamper his career.

If the line ends in a grille, it indicates lack of success. This indication is worse than a bar.

If the line ends in a grille on the Mount of Mercury, and there is a dot on the Mount of Apollo, the subject's status and prestige will suffer.

If the line ends in a fork (Fig. 98-NN), the native's efforts will be divided into two lines and he will fail to distinguish himself in either of them.

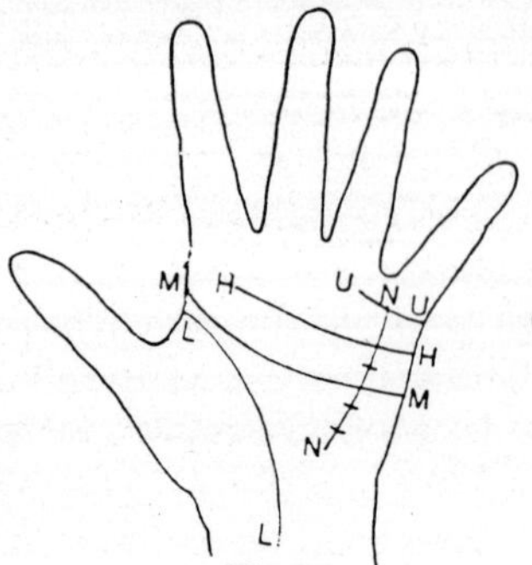

Fig 97

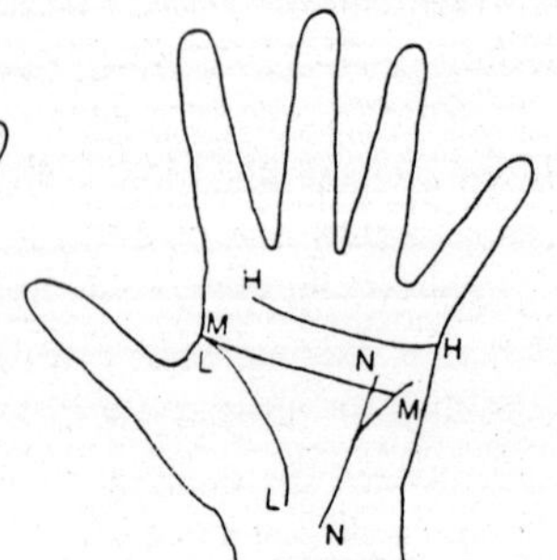

Fig 98

If the line ends in a star, the subject will achieve success in accordance with the length and the strength of the first (literary attainments), second (professional attainments), or third (business, trade, and commerce) phalanges of the Mercury finger.

If the line ends in a tassel, it indicates diffused efforts and, therefore, no success.

Defects

Whenever the Line of Health is defective in any manner, a corresponding examination should be made of the Lines of Life, Head, and Heart individually and jointly to see if ill health is indicated there too.

If the Line of Health is broad and shallow, it indicates lack of proper digestive powers and poor health. The subject will complain of lack of vitality and strength; he may have headaches, or other bilious complaints.

If the line is chained (Fig. 99-NN), it indicates a diseased liver; if the line is chained all throughout, the native may suffer from inflammation of the intestines, gall bladder, or ducts, or suffer from stones in the gall bladder, cirrhosis, etc. These diseases cause depression in the mind, making one pessimistic and melancholic in mental outlook.

If the line is wavy (Fig. 100-NN), it indicates chronic complaints of the liver. If the subject is Saturnine, he may suffer from rheumatism and nervous disorders; Jupiterean subjects are likely to suffer from gout; Apollonians from heart troubles;

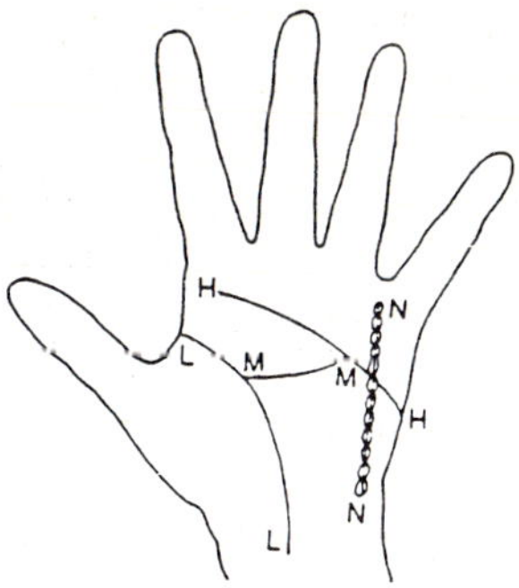

Fig 99

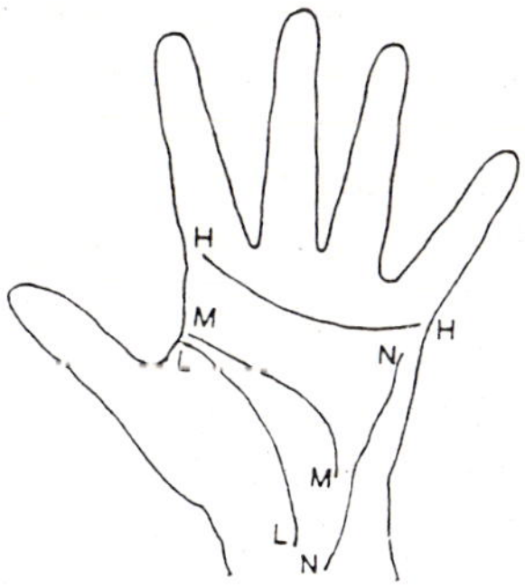

Fig 100

Mercurians from indigestion and nervousness. Subjects with an over-developed Mounts of Mars may suffer from inflammation of the intestines, or peptic ulcers. Those influenced by the Mount of Luna may be afflicted with gout, rheumatism, or dropsy, and Venusians, from bouts of fever.

In astrology, the planet Mercury is associated with the nervous system, speech, commerce, business, writing, travelling, liaising as an intermediary between two parties, and so on. When the Line of Health is defective, chained, wavy, ladder-like, full of islands, broken, or cut by small bars, the impact of the Mercurian qualities is reduced to a great extent. Ancient palmists have identified the line with trade and commerce, and if the line is defective, the subject cannot achieve complete success in any of the Mercurian occupations mentioned above.

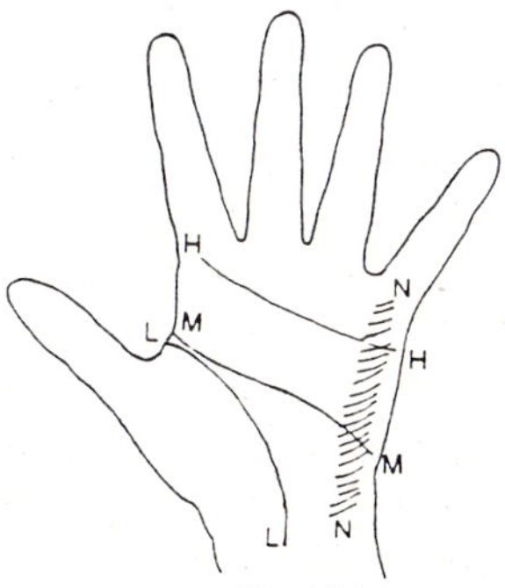

Fig 101

When the line is ladder-like (Fig. 101-NN), the native suffers from inflammation of the bowels, gastric fevers, etc. Health will always be a problem area.

Marks on the Line

A Coloured Dot: A coloured dot (Fig. 96-NN) on the Line of Health shows stomach disorders at the age it appears on the line. If the dot is red and deeply coloured, the effect is worse; in addition to stomach trouble, it indicates high fever. If a line from such a dot goes to any of the mounts, the disease will pertain to the planet on whose mount that line terminates. A white dot is bad, but a red dot is worse. Apart from a dot, if there are any other defects on the Line of Health, or if an off-shoot goes to any of the mounts, or if one of the mounts is defective (having grilles or other defects), the following diseases are indicated with respect to the given mounts:

Jupiter: the subject will suffer from diseases due to gluttony, particularly if the third phalange of the first finger is puffy and flabby.

Saturn: fever, rheumatism, melancholia, dyspepsia.

Apollo: heart trouble if the Line of Heart has an island, otherwise—diseases of the eyes. The nails should also be examined to analyse if there is a danger of heart disease.

Mercury: gastric trouble, fever.

Mars: inflammation of the intestines, appendicitis.

Luna: gout or stomach trouble.

Venus: fevers, spermatorrhoea in case of men; whites in case of females.

Cross-bars: Cross-bars cutting the Line of Health (Fig. 97-NN) show diseases at the ages the line is cut. If the cutting line is short and feeble, the disease will not be severe. But if the cutting line is deep and pronounced, it indicates a severe disease. If, in addition, there are many fine bars cutting the Line of Head and Health, they are the cause of headaches, or nervous trouble.

An Island: An island on the Line of Health (Fig. 95-NN) is a serious defect, and the subject will suffer from ill health during the age covered by the island. Two or three islands on the line show diseases of the throat and lungs. There are palmists who associate an island on the Line of Health with bankruptcy because this line also stands for trade and commerce.

A Break: A break in the line shows ill health or illness. If the line is broken at several places (Fig. 102-NN), it indicates chronic ill health of the body or the mind. If there is a repair line, or if the two ends of the broken line overlap, or if the broken ends are enclosed by a square, the defect is considerably remedied.

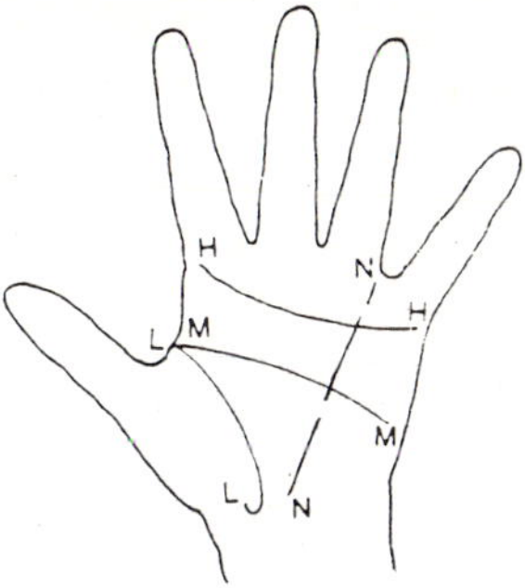

Fig 102

A Star: A star on the junction of the Line of Health and Line of Head in a female hand alludes to serious trouble connected with menstruation, ovaries, and the womb. In a male hand such a star is indicative of serious nervous trouble, schizophrenia, and so on. However, if the Lines of Head and Health are good, not only will there be no trouble, but also the subject will possess a brilliant intellect.

14

Minor Lines of the Hand
Lines of Influence

The thin lines (at times short, and at times very long) which originate from the Mount of Venus, or the Lower Mount of Mars, or from the Line of Life are categorised together as the Lines of Influence. Some on the Mount of Venus are in the form of concentric circular lines (Fig. 103-II), or straight slanting lines crossing the Line of Life and proceeding beyond it (Fig. 104-II).

Sometimes the hand appears to be full of many thin lines. In some hands many thin lines are cut across by other fine lines.

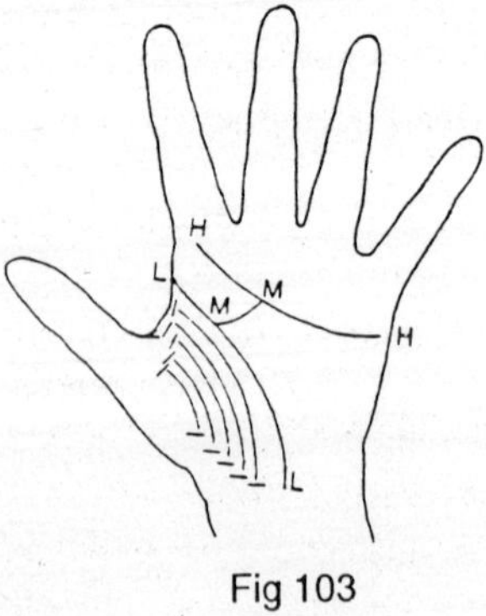

Fig 103

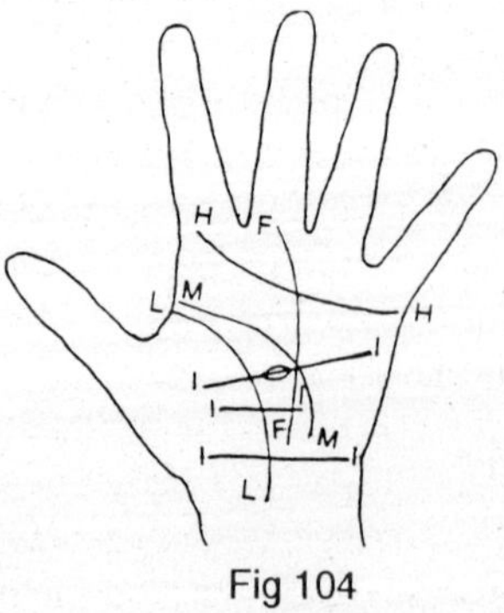

Fig 104

Interpretation for each of them is difficult to make beyond saying that they indicate a very sensitive and nervous temperament.

Characteristics

Most Lines of Influence stem from the Mount of Venus, Lower Mars, or the Line of Life. Sometimes, the lines, instead of being straight or oblique, are concentric on the Mount of Venus. The Line of Mars is also on the Mount of Venus but this is rather straight or, if curved, is only slightly curved. This is, in a way, also a Line of Influence but its chief effect is related to the plane of health. We shall deal with it in detail in a subsequent chapter.

Wavy Line: A wavy Line of Influence starting from the Mount of Venus and going to the Mount of Apollo (Fig. 105-II) indicates obstacles or some impediment in the way of success. If, instead of ending on the Mount of Apollo, it ends on the Mount of Mercury, the subject's progress in the field of commerce or exact sciences will be hindered.

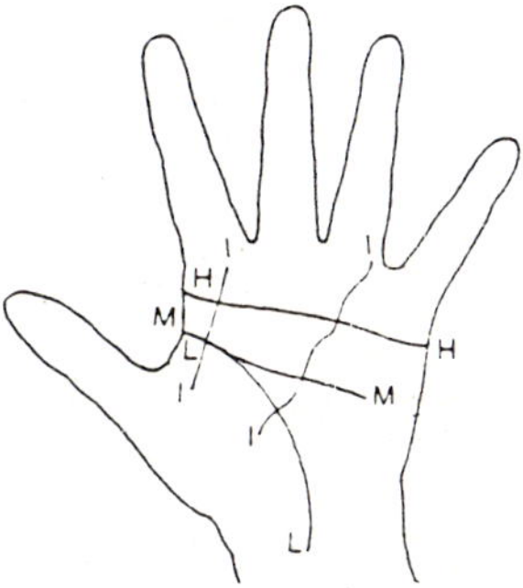

Fig 105

Concentric Lines: When the Lines of Influence are concentric, they indicate emotional influence. The greater the number of these concentric lines, the larger the number of people who influence the subject. Also, the closer they are to the Line of Life, the more intimate will be the influence. By their very position, being confined to the Mount of Venus, they cannot go to any other mount on the palm. But all these lines should be studied and the following inferences drawn:

1. If the Lines of Influence are deeply marked and complete (in the form of a sector of a circle), they show continuous influence over that period of life which they cover on the Line of Life (age to be reckoned on the Line of Life).

2. If the line is cut at places, the influence on the subject will be discontinued during the period it is cut.

3. If a line is near some portion of the Line of Life, and the same line gradually moves away from the Line of Life, it means that the persons who have a deep influence on the subject will be more intimate during the period that the Line of Influence is close to the Line of Life. They will drift away from him when the Line of Influence stands distant from the Line of Life.

Short, Oblique Line: When the Line of Influence is a short, oblique line across the Lower Mount of Mars, it denotes a love affair.

When a Line of Influence is on the Lower Mount of Mars, and ends in two or three branches on the Line of Life, it may allude to an overpowering influence of the beloved which could become a source of oppression to the subject.

Course of the Lines

Lines of Influence Stemming from the Mount of Venus or Lower Mars and Coming to the Line of Life: The Line of Influence which starts from the Lower Mount of Mars and meets the Line of Life indicates an influence on the child in his early years. This influence can be of the father, mother, nurse, or some other family member. At the stage (age to be reckoned on the Line of Life) the Line of Influence touches the Line of Life, its effect ceases to be felt. But if this Line of Influence starts from a star, it shows that some tragic event or bereavement is connected with the cessation of influence.

If the Line of Influence has an island on it (Fig. 104-II), it points to an intrigue by, or illness of the person who is exercising influence. Similarly, marks of a star or a cross should be interpreted as health troubles or some financial trouble to the party exercising influence upon the subject.

If the Line of Influence is broken, it indicates the discontinuity of the influence of another person on the subject at that point. If there are many breaks on the Line of Influence, the indication is of continuity of influence but with occasional breaks.

Before going any further, some important points should be kept in mind. The Lines of Influence emanating from the Mount of Venus must have some Venusian characteristics. In Western countries, where courtship is a normal affair, the influencing person may well be one of the opposite sex.

Another point of importance is that the influence of love on the positive side could mean increased attraction and attachment; on the negative side it could imply loss of affection due to death or separation.

Any lines arising out of Lower Mars, Venus, or the Line of Life, and proceeding in an oblique direction are evil (the general principle is that the upright lines are good, while horizontal or oblique lines, particularly those cutting the main lines, are harmful). If a well-marked oblique line cuts all the three major lines—the Line of Life, Head, and Heart—it indicates sorrow or bereavement. If it cuts the Lines of Life and Head only but not the Line of Heart, it is not so damaging; it indicates difficulties and worries, but no major tragedy.

Such lines cutting the Line of Fate (Fig. 104-II, FF) obstruct, diminish, or undermine the subject's fortune, that is, they are unfavourable for the subject financially.

Let us now revert to the quality of the Line of Influence.

When the Line of Influence coming from the Line of Life has many hair lines (very thin and fine lines), then it means that the influencing person himself is under the influence of others; so if the influencing person is a lover, his/her love will not be spontaneous—something will hinder it.

If there is more than one Line of Influence emanating from the Mount of Venus and touching the Line of Life, it can be predicted that there is more than one influence on the life of the subject.

What needs to be emphasized is that each Line of Influence should be examined individually; both its strength and drawbacks should be analysed, and the age (to be reckoned on the Line of Life) at the stage where it actually touches or comes near the Line of Life is to be taken into consideration.

Lines of Influence which Reach/Cut the Major Lines: Lines of Influence which go to other lines can be divided into two groups:

1. Lines of Influence which go to the other principal lines—Lines of Life, Head, Heart, and Fate—but stop short of meeting them and do not cut them.

2. Lines of Influence which cut the main lines:

If a Line of Influence cuts the Line of Life and terminates at the Line of Fate, it signals a love affair at the age it cuts the Line of Life or interference in the career of the subject (due to the line meeting the Line of Fate). If the line slightly cuts the Line of Fate, it means interference by friends and relations in the career of the subject and a consequent break in it.

A Line of Influence crossing the Line of Life and just touching the Line of Head, but not crossing it, points to interference by others in the mental freedom of the subject; but if the line cuts the Line of Head, it signifies a great deal of mental disturbance to the native due to the influence and interference of others.

A Line of Influence cutting the Lines of Life and Head, and merging in the Line of Heart is indicative of heart trouble (physical or mental or both) due to the conduct of a loved one. If such a line cuts the Line of Heart, the troubles will be compounded.

When a Line of Influence cuts the Line of Life, and an off-shoot goes upwards from the Line of Life, Line of Fate, and Heart and ends in the Mount of Mercury, that line is harmful since it cuts four lines, and denotes a love affair or marriage ending in death or divorce. Such a line impedes the subject's progress in life and fortune, because the off-shoot of the Line of Life and the Line of Fate is cut. The cutting of the Lines of Head and Heart indicates misfortune in love, mental shock (Line of Head), and shock to the heart (Line of Heart). If the Line of Influence cuts the Line of Union, it is a sure indication of separation or divorce. Otherwise the subject may face a troubled married life or separation.

A line cutting the Lines of Life, Fate, Head, and Apollo and ending in the Mount of Upper Mars denotes a wound on the head.

If the line proceeding towards any of the mounts under the base of the finger is not oblique but horizontal—moving from the Mount of Venus towards the Mount of Luna—it will naturally cut the Lines of Life and Fate, and is, as such, unfortunate. Both Venus (the commencing point) and Luna (the terminal point) are considered feminine planets and govern the influence of the opposite sex.

A Line of Influence from Venus merging with the Line of Apollo points to a rise in life due to the patronage or help of an influential party. But if the Line of Influence commences from the starting point of the Line of Life and cuts the Line of Apollo, it is unfortunate; it shows loss in financial affairs, social prestige, and honour at the age where the Line of Influence starts. If it is at too early an age, the subject's father or parents will be the victim of the financial disaster, because the subject will be too young to have any financial status of his own.

Any Line of Influence cutting the Line of Apollo is harmful. The Line of Apollo stands for honour and social prestige, and a line cutting it will mean that these will suffer due to the influence of others. If the cut is deep, and the Line of Apollo disappears, or becomes broken or indistinct, it means a great scandal will ruin the subject's reputation. It should be borne in mind that the cutting of the Line of Apollo has a negative effect, but merging with it is considered good.

A Line of Influence cutting the Line of Union indicates divorce. If the Line of Union has a fork and the Line of Influence merges with one of the prongs, the effect is the same.

If the Line of Influence has an island on it, the divorce will be due to a love affair.

Lines Ending in the Triangle: The area enclosed by the Lines of Life, Head, and Health is called the Triangle. Several oblique Lines of Influence commencing from the Mount of Venus or Lower Mars, and cutting the Line of Life, but not the Line of Fate or Head, represent annoyance or worries due to interference in the affairs of the subject by the people who exert influence over him. Since these Lines of Influence do not cut the Lines of Fate or Head, their effect is confined to causing worries and annoyance. If the lines are numerous, thin and fine, they show a nervous disposition. But if, instead of many fine hair lines or a few marked oblique lines, there is a very deep and strong line from the Mount of Venus which cuts the Line of Life, it indicates a bereavement due to the death of a beloved, or some cruel or unfaithful conduct by him. If such a line rises from the first phalange of the thumb and crosses the Line of Life, it indicates death in a fight. There is also an apprehension that the person might be assassinated.

A semi-circular line cutting the Line of Life shows serious illness or even death if other prognostications confirm it.

Lines Ending in Mounts: Some Lines of Influence commence from the Mount of Venus or Lower Mars, cross the Line of Life, and go to the mounts.

A line emanating from the junction of the Line of Life and Head, going to the Mount of Jupiter, then turning horizontally, and ending in the Mount of Saturn indicates religiousness.

A line from the Mount of Venus to the Mount of Jupiter (Fig. 105-II) signifies ambition and success. If such a line ends in a star on the Mount of Jupiter, these characteristics are strengthened. But if it ends in a bar or is cut by a bar, it becomes weak.

A line from the Mount of Venus, going to the Mount of Saturn, and acting like a sister line to the Line of Fortune promises increase in wealth due to the influence, help, or patronage of others; the same effect is felt if, instead of commencing from the Mount of Venus, the line commences from the Mount of Luna. If the line commencing from the Mount of Venus or Luna does not end in the Mount of Saturn but goes to the third phalange of the second finger, then it is bad. In a female hand it may threaten trouble in child bearing or delivery.

A line from Venus to the Mount of Saturn could allude to an accident, particularly so, if the line ends in a fork, cross, or a grille. Sometimes it refers to marital discord. During its course, if this line also cuts an off-shoot from the Line of Life, separation or divorce is likely to result.

If a Line of Influence from the Mount of Venus goes to the Mount of Apollo or Mercury without being cut by any other lines, or without any defects at its commencement or at the end, the subject will be successful in his career due to the help or patronage of others.

Marks on the Lines

We shall now deal with the characteristics of the Lines of Influence which have some marks such as a star, an island, or a dot on them.

Star: A line from Venus which has a star at its commencement, proceeds towards the Line of Life and cuts it, signifies bereavement.

A line which commences on the Mount of Venus and cuts an off-shoot of the Line of Life means that the prospects of progress in the subject's life and career are cut short due to the influence of another person. For example, a person may have good prospects in a foreign country, but his parents may not allow him to go abroad; or a person may be transferred on promotion to a distant place, but he may not avail the opportunity due to his wife's insistence that he should not go abroad. This cutting of the Line of Life and its off-shoot also leads to bereavement and loss.

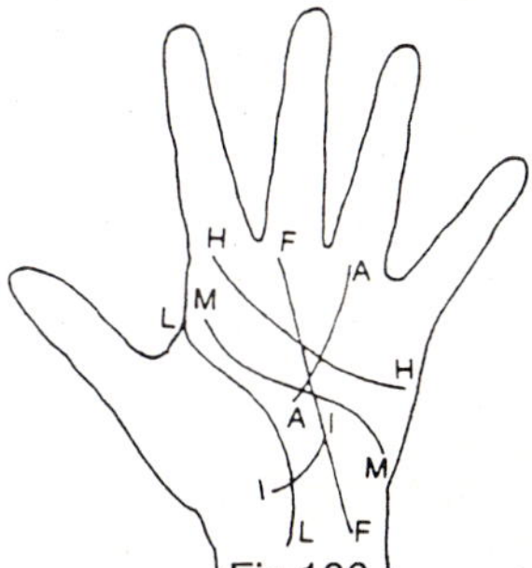

Fig 106

If such a Line of Influence merges with the Line of Fate or the Line of Apollo (Fig. 106-II, FF), making the line with which it merges, stronger after the merger takes place—it can be construed as a good omen, predicting increase in fortune or fame as the case may be. It is probable that such a rise in fortune may be the result of the death of one of the relatives of the subject. But if such a Line of Influence simply cuts the Line of Fate or Apollo (Fig. 107-II, FF, AA), it will nullify their good qualities, and instead, result in loss of wealth or status due to a bereavement.

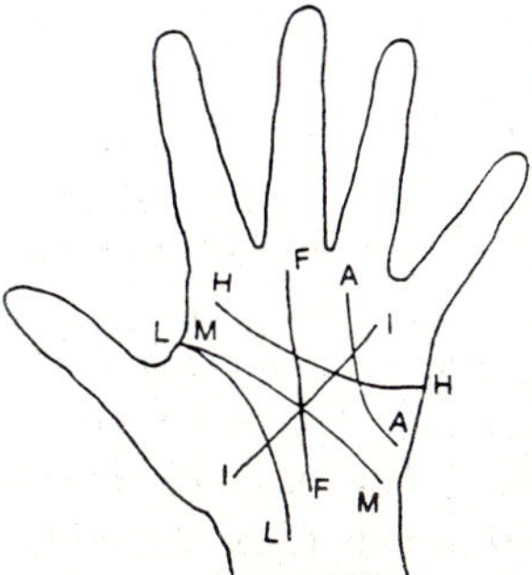

Fig 107

If the line cuts an off-shoot starting from the Line of Life and terminates at a star on the Line of Apollo, it is worse. The native's prospects in life will be spoiled due to loss incurred in a litigation or scandal.

If a line which starts on the Mount of Venus and ends in a fork on the Mount of Saturn has a star at the commencement of the line, the subject will face marital discord, resulting in a premature termination of the marriage. If the above line ends on the Mount of Apollo, the subject's life will be beset with bereavement, quarrels, and financial ruin.

A Line of Influence commencing from the Mount of Venus and ending in a star on the Mount of Jupiter (Fig. 108-II) is a good sign. It signifies ambition in the native and success in his enterprise.

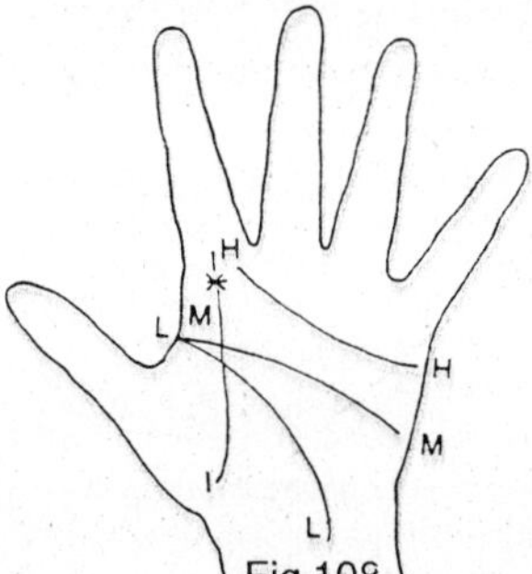

Fig 108

A line commencing on the Mount of Venus, cutting the Lines of Life and Fate, and ending in a star at the Plain of Mars shows heavy financial loss or ruin (age to be reckoned on the Line of Fate).

Two lines originating from two different positions on the Mount of Venus, and ending at the same point on the Line of Fate refer to two influences from two sources (may be love affairs, may be two partners in business). They will be responsible for ruining the financial prospects of the subject. The effect will be worse if there is a star on the Line of Fate at that point. If the Line of Fate is strong thereafter, the subject will recover from the financial loss, but if it stops or is feeble or cut, the native will not be able to recover from the disaster.

If a Line of Influence emanating from Venus ends in a star on the Line of Head or Heart, it indicates great mental worry (if it ends on the Line of Head) and heart disease, or shock caused by the death or conduct of a beloved person. (Age should be reckoned on the Line of Head as the case may be).

If there is a star at the commencement of the line as well as at its termination, and if the Line of Influence originates from the Mount of Venus and

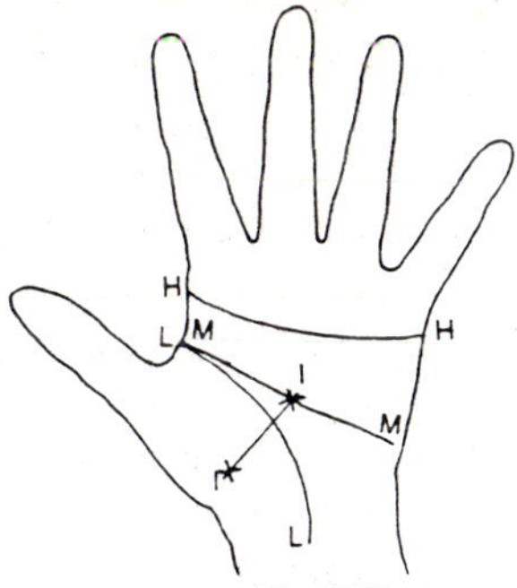

Fig 109

1. ends in the Plain of Mars, the subject will be hit by some bereavement and financial ruin;

2. ends on the Line of Head (Fig. 109-II, MM), a bereavement and great mental trouble will befall the native.

3. ends on the Line of Fate, the subject will be confronted with a loss of fortune due to some death;

4. ends on the Line of Apollo (Fig. 110-II, AA), it points to a scandal or loss of an important case.

5. ends on the Line of Heart (Fig. 111-II, HH), it is indicative of a bereavement or serious heart trouble.

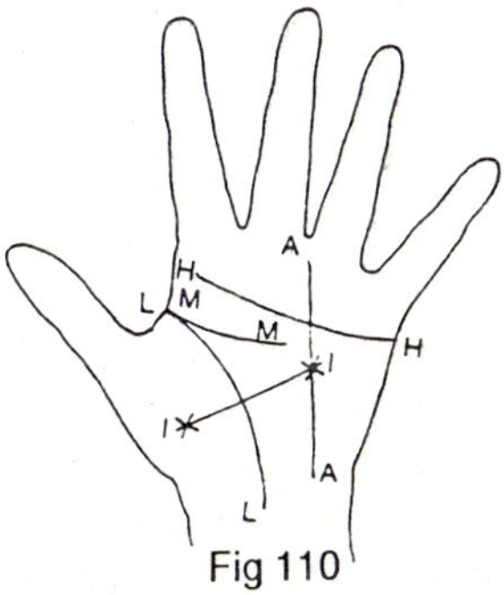

Fig 110

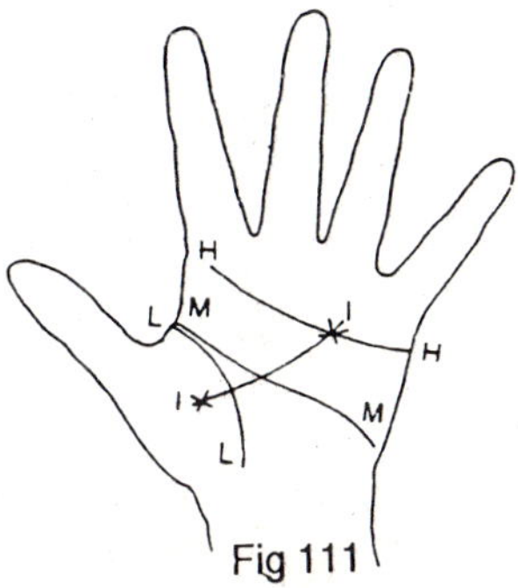

Fig 111

An Island: An island is also considered a bad mark. When a line from the Mount of Venus emanates from an island and goes to the Line of Life or beyond it, it is interpreted as a clandestine love affair. If such a line cuts the off-shoot springing from the Line of Life, it spoils the prospects of progress in life. If such a line merges with the Line of Fate or Apollo, the clandestine love affair will not adversely affect the fortunes and reputation of the subject, particularly, if the Line of Fate or

Apollo is good after the point of merger. But if, instead of merging with the Line of Fate and Apollo, the Line of Influence cuts them, it will have an adverse effect on the subject's fortune, (if it cuts the Line of Fate) or status and reputation (if it cuts the Line of Apollo). If such a line ends at the Lines of Head or Heart, it should be interpreted accordingly.

When a Line of Influence has no mark or sign at the commencement and ends in an island, it generally means that it does not meet any independent line at its terminating point; however, it splits into two, and then meets again forming an island. When such an islanded Line of Influence

1. ends in the Mount of Jupiter, it indicates illness either due to good living or due to want of fresh air, and respiratory troubles;

2. touches the Lines of Fate and Heart, the subject may have a clandestine love affair, or suffer from some financial misfortune or emotional shock;

3. ends in the Mount of Mercury, cutting the Lines of Fate and Apollo, a clandestine love affair may bring disgrace to the subject.

Stars and Islands: If a Line of Influence commences from the Mount of Venus with a star and ends in an island on the Line of Head (Fig. 112-II, MM), Heart, Fate, or Apollo, then it is an ominous sign showing death of a near and dear one. If there is an island at the beginning and an island at the termination of the Line of Influence, they indicate guilty intrigue and failure in life due to that. If, however, the line commences with an island on the Mount of Venus, and terminates in a star on the Line of Fate, it should be interpreted as ruining of fortune due to an external influence or a love affair. Such a line is harmful and should be interpreted as an adverse influence if it ends in the Line of Head, Heart, or Apollo.

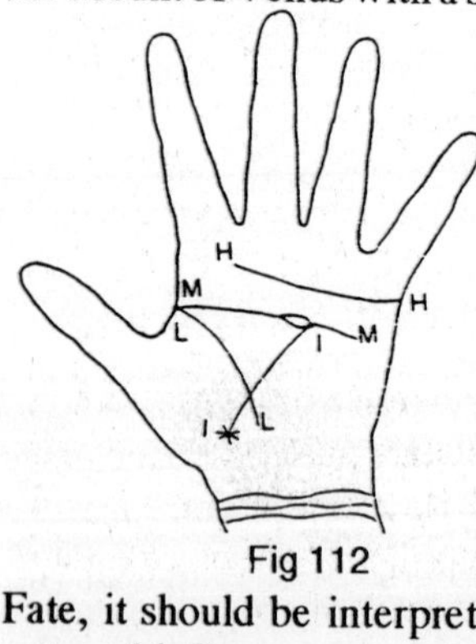

Fig 112

An island on a Line of Influence, with or without any star anywhere on it, indicates a clandestine love affair and misfortune due to it.

Dot: A dot at the commencement of a line on the Mount of Venus, or a Line of Influence originating from there and ending in a dot are both negative signs.

If a line commences from a dot, crosses the Line of Life, cutting an off-shoot going upwards from the latter; and if there is a cross on the Mount of Jupiter, it indicates a love marriage ending in a separation or divorce. It also has a derogatory effect on the future prospects of the subject.

If the line commences with a star on the Mount of Venus and ends in a dot on the Line of Head, then there is a strong possibility of severe affliction of the brain.

If a Line of Influence commences with a star on the Mount of Venus and ends in a dot on the Line of Fate (Fig. 113-II, FF), then it indicates misfortune in wealth or career due to some bereavement.

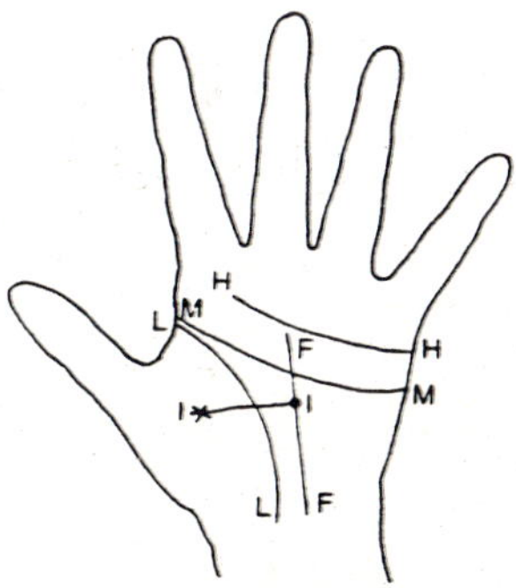

Fig 113

Fork: If a Line of Influence terminates at the Line of Heart and has a fork at its termination, it may allude to a separation due to an early death or divorce.

If, in addition to the above, there is an island on the Line of Fate, it signifies separation due to a clandestine love affair, as well as misfortune in a financial matter or the career.

If the line ends in a fork on the Mount of Saturn, it points to divorce.

In this way there can be many permutations and combinations of stars, islands, dots, and other marks. The termination points of the Lines of Influence can also be many. The point to remember is that any bad mark in the beginning or at the end, or at both the terminals is evil.

15

Minor Lines of the Hand
Lines of Union or Marriage

Small horizontal lines coming from the side of the hand on to the Mount of Mercury are called Lines of Marriage (Fig. 114-UU). However, interestingly—they have also been found on the hands of persons who have never married and died single. Many palmists refer to those lines as the Lines of Union or Lines of Affection. The union always refers to the sexual union with a member of the opposite sex—one which leaves an indelible mark on the subject's mind. The presence of more than one such 'line' may indicate more than one deep and lasting relationship. Frivolous affairs are not indicated by the Lines of Union. They can be read in the Line of Heart, Lines of Influence, and in the Girdle of Venus on hands in which the girdle is present. But deep and abiding passion, and sexual relations over a long period have to be identified with the Lines of Union or Marriage.

To obtain a complete picture of one's sexual life, the hand should be studied as a whole, particularly the shape of the hand, the Mounts of Venus and Mars, the principal lines, the Lines of Influence, and the Girdle of Venus. The study should not be confined to the Lines of Union alone.

Characteristics

It has often been observed that many married persons—even those with children—have a very faint Line of Union. A faint line, therefore, does not indicate that the subject will not get married. It merely means that such a person has passed his married life in a routine manner, and there has not been any deep attachment or ardent love between the couple. On the other hand, a long and deep line coming right up to the Mount of Mercury indicates the depth and intimacy of conjugal happiness.

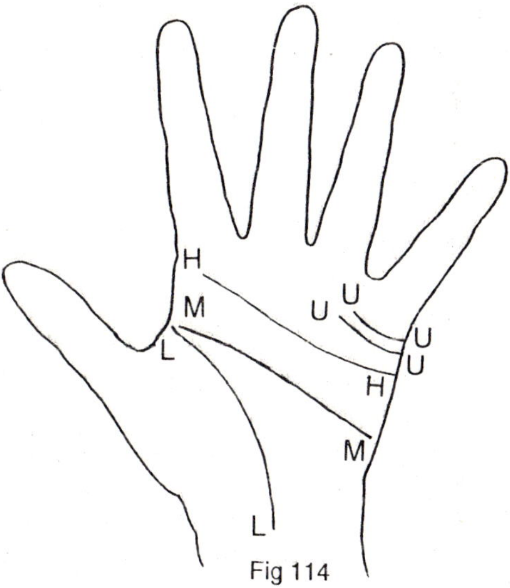

Fig 114

The effect and timings of marriage vary from one type of person to the other. Jupitereans, Venusians, Mercurians, and Martians like to marry at a young age. Saturnines do not have much warmth. Many of them do not marry, and those who marry, do so at a comparatively late age. People with a prominent Mount of Apollo look for a distinguished and brilliant partner who does not really fit into the domestic sphere, and, as such, their marriages are not very successful. Persons with a prominent Mount of Luna enter into a marriage, which is, in some way or other, peculiar.

A good and deep Line of Union is preferred to a thin or short line. Some palmists have given an age schedule according to the position of the Line of Union between the Line of Heart and the base of the Mercury finger. But in practice it has been found that this age schedule does not work well. The age of marriage among Indian girls and boys is rising, while in the United States of America, the age of marriage is coming down. Hence, calculations regarding the age of marriage are made in terms of i) early, ii) at an average age and iii) late. If the Line of Influence is near the Line of Heart, an early marriage is predicted; if in the middle—the subject will tie the marital knot at an average age; and if nearer the base of the fourth finger, a late marriage is likely. When there are two Lines of Union, and one line is nearer the Line of Heart and inclined towards it—it signifies that the spouse will die. A second, longer, and distinct line alludes to a second marriage.

Course of the Lines

According to one eminent palmist, if the Line of Union starts with a fork, it shows that the affection is of unusual strength: the two lines of the fork having united to form a single line. However, while examining hands, it has been found that the Line of Union, whether starting with a fork (Fig. 115-UU) or ending in a fork (Fig. 116-UU), indicates separation. When the fork is at the commencement (on the percussion), the separation or divorce is due to the subject's own fault; but when the fork is at the termination, the separation or divorce is due to the other person's fault.

If the Line of Union droops or turns towards the Line of Heart (Fig. 117-UU), it shows great disappointment or sorrow in love; either the affection does not culminate in marriage, or the beloved dies. If the Line of Union is located near the base of the Mercury finger, there is no sorrow and probably no marriage.

If the Line of Union turns towards the Line of Heart from the very beginning or at an early stage, then sorrow due to disappointment or death, will be at an early stage. But if the line is straight, and moves towards the Mount of Mercury up to a certain distance, and then inclines towards the Line of Heart, the

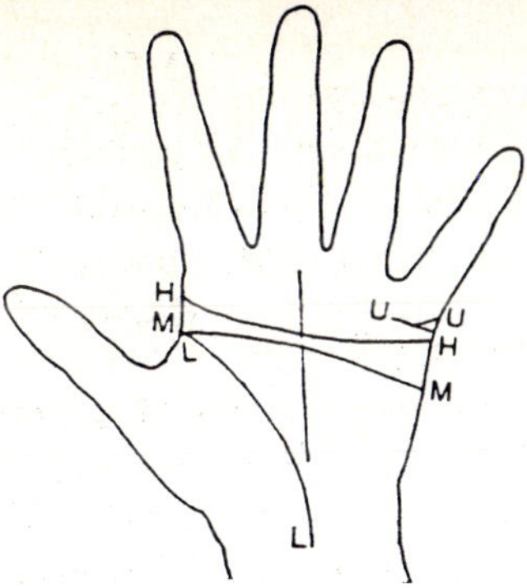

Fig 115

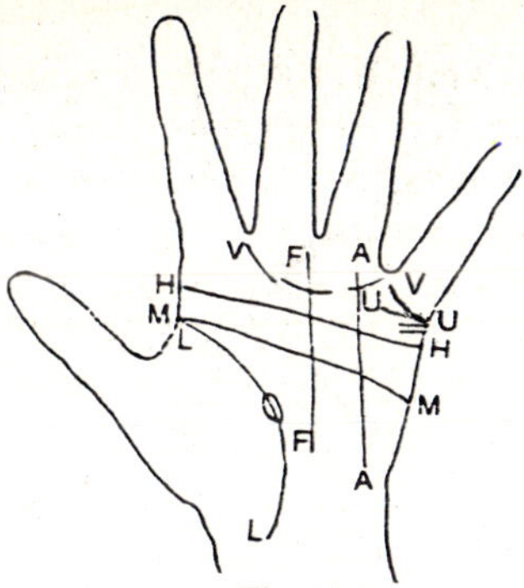

Fig 116

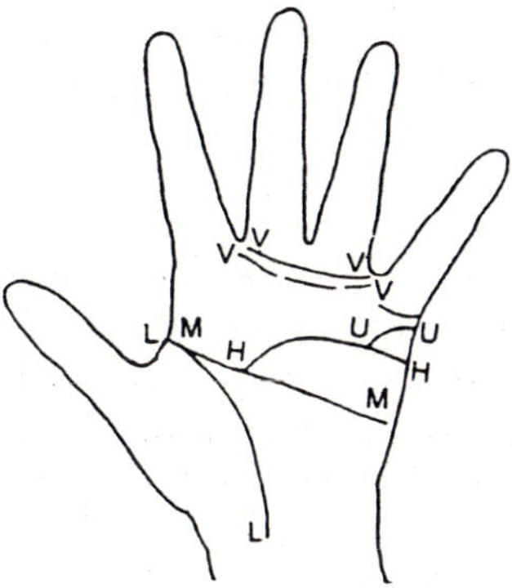

Fig 117

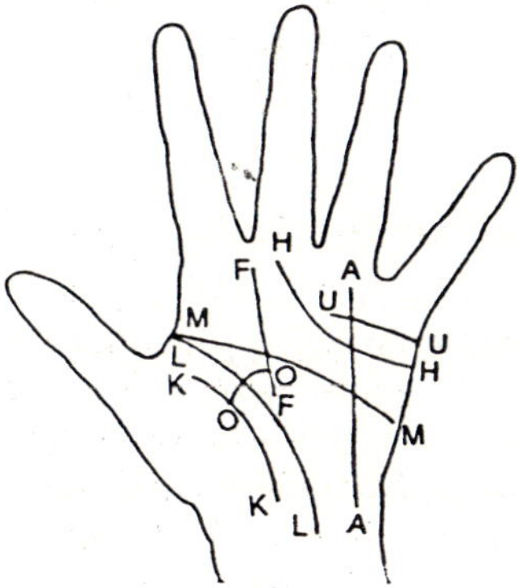

Fig 118

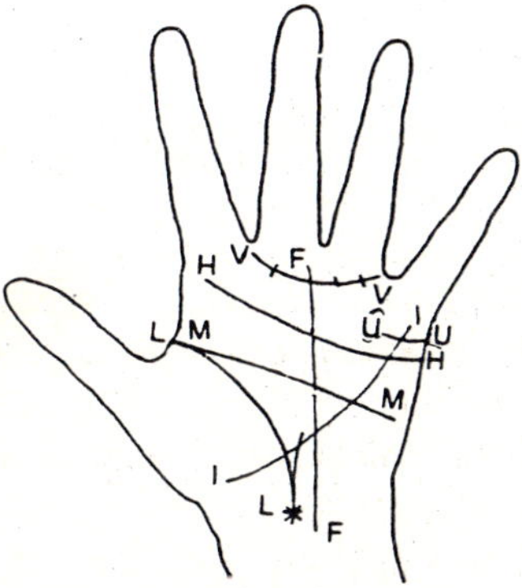

Fig 119

subject will experience sorrow rather late in life.

When the Line of Union touches the Line of Apollo, it is considered good. It indicates marriage or union with a person who is rich and famous. However if the line cuts the Line of Apollo, the marriage or union will have an adverse effect on the status of the subject (Fig. 118-UU).

Sometimes a Line of Influence arising from the Mount of Luna, and joining the Line of Apollo or Fate also indicates marriage with a person of status at the age (age to be reckoned on the Line of Apollo or Fate) at which the Line of Influence merges with the Line of Apollo or Fate.

Any Line of Influence from the Mount of Venus which cuts an off-shoot from the Line of Life and also cuts the Line of Union (Fig. 119-II, LL, UU), indicates separation or divorce. A Line of Influence commencing from the Triangle and cutting the Line of Union has the same effect.

Absence of the Lines

If the Line of Union is absent, one should look for other related indications. If the other features of the hand and lines show vigour and vitality, the native will satisfy himself by having extra-marital relationships. In such hands, any defects on the Line of Heart will indicate heart disease and not affairs of the heart.

Defects

If a line is deep and well-cut at the commencement, and becomes gradually thinner, it shows a gradual waning of love.

A break in the line represents a break in the marriage.

If the Line of Union is cut by straight lines on the Mount of Mercury (Fig. 119-UU), there will be impediments in the marriage or union.

Marks on the Lines

A Black Spot: A black spot on the Line of Union signifies widowhood.

An Island: An island on the line symbolizes quarrels with the beloved or an intrigue.

A Cross: A cross alludes to impediments.

A Star: A star at the end of the line points to a sudden end of the relationship due to death or divorce.

Girdle of Venus

While the Line of Union signifies affection, the Girdle of Venus points to the sensuous side of the subject (Fig. 120). This line is found in a few hands only. If it is found, it commences between the bases of the fingers of Jupiter and Saturn and ends between the fingers of Apollo and Mercury. It is a curved line bulging towards the palm. The line may be complete or broken. In some hands there are several lines parallel to each other, complete or broken (Fig. 117-VV). In some hands the line rises on the Mount of Jupiter and ends on the Mount of Mercury.

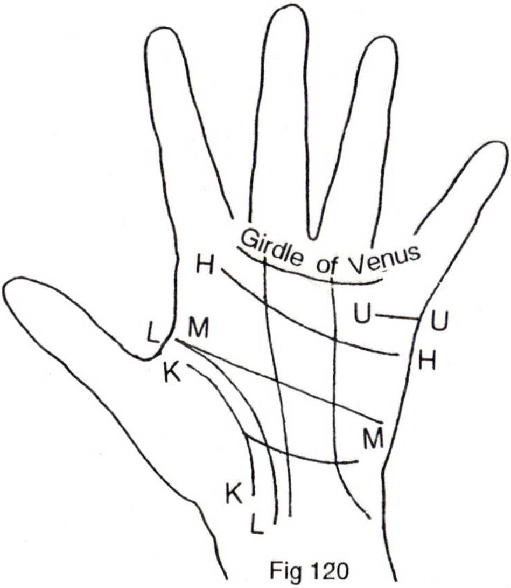

Fig 120

This line is interpreted by many palmists as a sister line to the Line of Heart and, as such, stands for emotions. But the emotions are chiefly confined to the domain of sex. Subjects having this line are highly sensuous, with strong sexual desires. They have frequent love affairs and have no scruples about being licentious. A complete Girdle of Venus is not as bad as one which is broken. It denotes increased sensuality. Double or triple lines (Girdles of Venus) increase sensuousness, but if they are broken, the sexual side shows unhealthy development. In an otherwise good hand, a complete line bestows energy and ardour on the subject, but in a bad hand, it indicates licentiousness.

If this Girdle cuts the Line of Fate or Apollo, it is to be interpreted as an obstacle to earning wealth, or gaining a position due to sexual aberrations. At the stage where it cuts the Line of Union, it destroys marital happiness. While interpreting the cutting of any line by the Girdle, it should be borne in mind that loss in wealth, rank, or conjugal happiness will be due to the abnormal sexual nature of the subject. In many women's hands, it denotes that their sexual urges and abnormalities do not find satisfaction in their partners, and this gives rise to nervousness, hysteria, and allied problems.

If the Girdle is cut by many short lines, (Fig. 119-VV), it increases bad qualities. If it is cut by a line on the Mount of Saturn, it indicates loss of wealth. If it is cut on the Mount of Apollo, it means loss of position, and so on. A star on the Girdle is indicative of venereal diseases.

16

Additional Minor Lines

Line of Mars

The Line of Mars is on the Mount of Venus and, generally, runs parallel to the Line of Life, though it is not as long as the latter. It is treated as a sister line to the Line of Life (Fig. 121-KK), if there are any defects on the Line of Life, or it is faded or indistinct. If the corresponding portion on the Line of Mars is well formed and clear cut, then the subject suffering from ill health or diseases due to the deficiencies and bad marks on the Line of Life will recover. In other words, the Line of Mars acts as a protecting line. It is not found on all hands. If the Line of Life has a break or any other serious defects, then the absence of the Line of Mars means lack of a protecting influence for the defects.

Being located on the Mount of Venus, it should also be considered as a Line of Influence. Its influence is, however, confined mainly to health. Since it commences from the Lower Mount of Mars, it is called the Line of Mars. If the line is short and runs parallel to the Line of Life only for a short distance, its influence is confined to that portion of the Line of Life which is covered by it.

In this connection it is necessary to sound a note of warning. Many Western palmists have referred to love affairs, intrigues, and extra-marital relationships in the context of the Line of Mars, Line of Heart, and so on, because in Western societies, they are frequent occurrences, while in India, moral values tend to be relatively traditional. Social conditions should, therefore, be kept in mind while making such predictions.

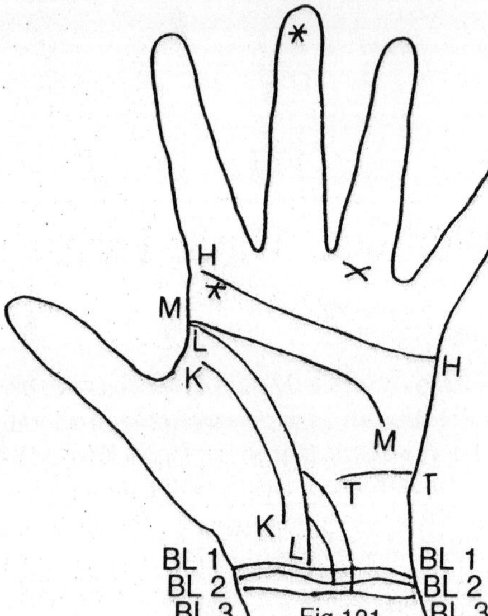

Fig 121

If the Line of Mars ends in a fork, and one prong goes to the Mount of Luna (Fig. 120-KK), it shows intemperate habits. If there is a star at the end of the fork on the Mount of Mars, it is still worse. The subject may turn out to be a drunkard.

Off-shoots from the Line of Mars: Off-shoots from the Line of Mars going to the Line of Life and merging in it are indications of progress.

If an off-shoot from the Line of Mars goes to the Line of Head and merges with it (Fig. 122-KK, OO, MM), the subject will be mentally strong at that age (age to be reckoned on the Line of Head).

An off-shoot from the Line of Mars merging with the Line of Fate (Fig. 118-KK, OO, FF) strengthens fortune (age to be reckoned on the Line of Fate).

In the cases given above, if instead of merging with the lines, the off-shoots cut them, the effect is harmful. In fact, any off-shoots from the Line of Mars going to the Line of Heart or Apollo are good; but any off-shoots cutting the Line of Apollo, Heart, or Union are harmful and produce adverse effects pertaining to the line they cut.

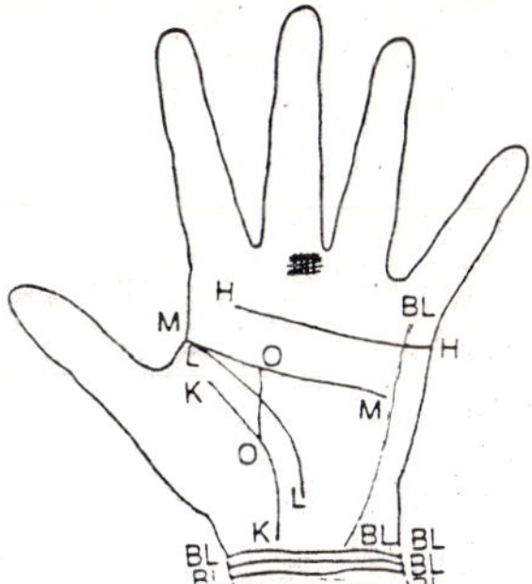

Fig 122

Ring of Solomon

The Ring of Solomon is a small semi-circular line, rising from between the bases of the first and second finger and encircling the Mount of Jupiter (Fig. 123-SS). It indicates a love for the occult sciences.

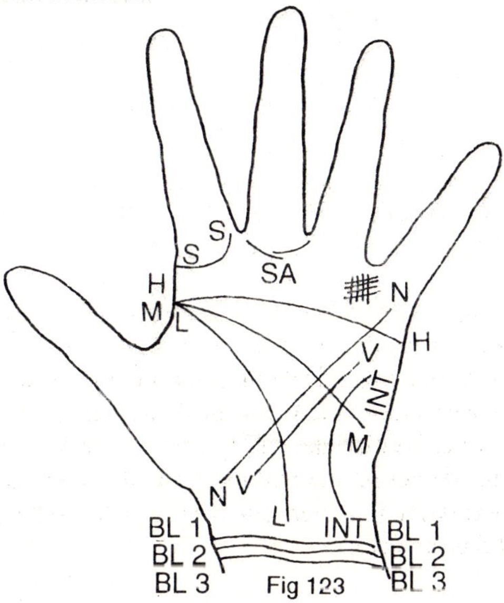

Fig 123

Ring of Saturn

The Ring of Saturn is a small-circular line rising from between the bases of the first and second fingers and encircling the base of the second finger (Fig. 123-SA).

It indicates a change of occupation. The native leaves one career for another. If the ring has a break, he is even less persevering.

Via Lascivia

This line is found in very few hands (Fig. 123-VV). When it is found, it is generally parallel to the Line of Health. It originates from the Mount of Luna or the space between the Lines of Life and Health, and if it is long, it ends in the Mount of Mercury; if short, on the Lower Mount of Luna.

As the name Lascivia indicates, the line stands for lasciviousness. Lascivious means lustful and wanton. The subject will either have great lust for money or for pleasure. If the line starts from the Mount of Venus, it makes one immoral. If the line is wavy, the native will have many love affairs.

Via Lascivia acts as a sister line to the Line of Health. If the latter is defective at any stage, and a good line of Via Lascivia runs parallel to the defective portion of the Line of Health, it counteracts the harm caused by the defects just as a good Line of Mars protects the Line of Life.

If it ends at the Mount of Mercury, it brings good luck and inculcates some good qualities of the Mount of Mercury. But if it ends in a fork, the subject is indolent and wastes his life in pleasures.

Any upward branches from it merging with the Line of Apollo indicate wealth and honour; but if the off-shoots cut the Line of Apollo, they indicate disgrace and loss of wealth.

Whenever a defect is found on any of the principal lines (Lines of Life, Head, Fate, and Heart, and the Via Lascivia is present, the defect on the main line should be explained as a result of excessive indulgence in pleasures due to the sensuous nature of the subject.

Line of Intuition

The Line of Intuition is rare and is found only in a few hands. It rises on the Mount of Luna and curves (the convex side towards the Line of Apollo), ending on or near the Mount of Mercury (Fig. 123-INT).

Subjects who have this line are gifted with powers of intuition. Naturally, such a line in a square hand will not provide the same level of intuition as on a psychic hand. Another point which should also be kept in mind is that a woman, generally, has more intuitive powers than a man.

Other factors in the hand which add to intuitive or psychic powers are i) a well-developed Mount of Luna; ii) a Line of Head which slopes towards the Mount of Luna; iii) long fingers with pointed tips, and iv) a pointed thumb.

The general principle is that if the Line of Intuition is long, unbroken, and without defects, it will provide greater intuitive powers than a short or broken line. If the Line of Intuition cuts the Line of Head, it damages the power of the brain.

The Bracelets

Bracelets are lines on the inner side of the wrist (where the hand is joined to the arm) (Fig. 124-BL1, BL2, BL3). These are also called *rascettes.* It is good to have three unbroken bracelets. If the wrist is firm and fleshy, it augurs a long life and wealth; but if it is weak and lean, it indicates poverty. If these bracelets have small, longish islands of the shape of barley, the subject is usually rich. According to the Hindu science of palmistry, if there are three such bracelets, the subject becomes a king. If there are two of such a description, the subject is very intelligent and holds a rank equal to that of a minister. If these bracelets are not only on the inside of the palm but extend all round the wrist evenly, it is still better. Ladies with such bracelets wear costly jewellery round their wrists.

The bracelet nearest the hand is referred to as the first bracelet, and the one which is farthest, as the third bracelet. The middle one is referred to as the second bracelet. If the first bracelet is broken, it bodes premature death. If the second

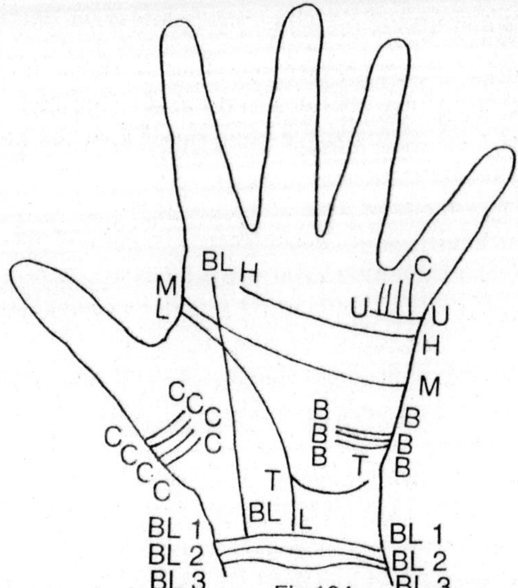

Fig 124

bracelet is broken, the subject dies before he reaches old age; and when the third bracelet is broken, death in old age is predicted. Only when all the three bracelets are good and unbroken, does the native die at a ripe old age. This judgement, however, must be corroborated by the state and condition of the Line of Life too. Some other inferences drawn from these bracelets are:

1. If the first bracelet bulges towards the base of the palm (Fig. 124-BL1) in female hands, it signifies trouble in child bearing. In male hands, it is indicative of some drawbacks in fecundity or matters of sex.

2. A line from the first bracelet to the Mount of Jupiter (Fig. 124-BL) is a sign of a fruitful and long journey. If there is also a cross on the bracelet, the journey will be a success monetarily.

3. If two lines from the first bracelet go to the Mount of Saturn and cross each other, they are a warning of mishaps in a long journey.

4. A line from the first bracelet going to the Mount of *Apollo* indicates honour and wealth;

Mercury is a sign of the subject suddenly acquiring wealth (Fig. 122-BL);

Luna points to a long journey;

5. Lines from the bracelets ending on the Line of Life (Fig. 121-BL, LL) are a warning of death on a journey or death abroad;

6. A wavy line from the bracelet cutting the Line of Health is an indication of bad health and ill luck;

7. A triangle with a cross inside, or a star, or the mark of an angle on the bracelet indicates inheritance.

Line of Travel

When the Line of Life is split at its end into two and one branch goes to the Mount of Luna (Fig. 124-TT, LL), it indicates travel.

A horizontal line across the Mount of Luna also indicates foreign travel (Fig. 121-TT).

A line from the first bracelet to the Mount of Jupiter indicates a sea voyage. Lines starting from the bracelet and going to the Mount of Luna also indicate a long journey.

Some additional points are being given below:

1. When a Line of Travel meets the Line of Fate and merges with it, and the Line of Fate becomes stronger after the merger, it indicates an increase in fortune due to the voyage; but if it cuts the Line of Fate and the latter becomes weak, the effect is the reverse.

2. A cross at the end of a Line of Travel denotes disappointment, implying that the voyage may prove to be unfruitful.

3. A square on a Line of Travel, as on any other line, is indicative of protection.

4. It is good for a Line of Travel to proceed from the bracelet and then go on the Mount of Jupiter, Apollo, or Mercury, but bad if it goes to the Mount of Saturn.

Accidents are connected with the Mount of Saturn if there is an island on it, and a line from the island comes to the Line of Life, and cuts it. If the line from the island does not cut the Line of Life, the accident will not be serious. Similarly, if there is an island on the Mount of Saturn, and any line from it cuts the Lines of Head or Heart, the subject will suffer from brain or heart damage. However if the line only touches the Lines of Head or Heart, the severity of the damage is far reduced.

If any line starts from the base of the Mount of Saturn and cuts the Line of Life, it indicates an accident while on a journey.

5. If an off-shoot from a Line of Travel goes to the lower side (towards the base of the hand), then it does not augur well, but if the off-shoot goes towards a mount, it is a good sign—except if it goes to the Mount of Saturn.

Thus it can be seen that there can be many permutations and combinations according to various marks or signs at the beginning, in the middle, or at the end of the Line of Travel.

Lines of Children

According to the Hindu texts (which we follow, and the findings of which have been confirmed by experience), a line or lines at the base of the Mount of Venus (where the lower portion of the thumb ends) towards the Line of Life (Fig.124 -CC) indicate children. The thicker lines indicate sons, the thinner ones, daughters. Lines which are complete indicate children who will have a reasonably long span, life while broken lines indicate that children will die prematurely.

According to Western palmistry, vertical lines on the Line of Union or Marriage (Fig. 124-C) stand for children, the thicker ones for sons, the thinner ones for daughters. Broken or cut lines indicate children who will die prematurely. These fine lines are generally not visible except when viewed through a magnifying glass.

Lines of Brothers and Sisters: These are indicated by lines arising from the percussion on the Mount of Upper Mars and Luna (Fig. 124-BB). Here also, thick lines indicate brothers, and finer lines, sisters. Very small lines indicate brothers and sisters with a short life.

17

Significant Markings on the Palm and Fingers

The description of the marks and signs such as a star, grille, cross-bar, cross, and so on have been given in previous chapters dealing with the lines of the hand. These marks have a definite significance in connection with the line when found on any of the mounts or in the quadrangle, or on any of the fingers or the thumb. Though generally described as producing ill effects, these marks may actually produce good effects in certain places.

A Star

A Star on the Mount of

Jupiter indicates that the subject is very ambitious and will be able to fulfil his ambitions; he will rise beyond his expectations in life (Fig. 121).

Saturn points to paralysis. If the Line of Fate goes to the third phalange, there is danger of the subject having murderous tendencies.

Apollo alludes to wealth, name, and fame if the Line of Apollo is good as well.

Mercury denotes a high level of intelligence

Upper Mars is a sign of uncontrollable anger if the mount is overdeveloped. If the mount is normal, the subject may face death due to an injury.

Luna shows that there may be a danger of drowning; if the star is on the lower one-third part of the mount, sufferance due to ascites[1] is likely.

Venus indicates a death in the family. If the star is near the thumb, it denotes an intrigue, and an all-absorbing love affair. If there is a star near the Line of Life, and a sloping Line of Head goes down to the Mount of Luna, the subject is endowed with a powerfully erotic imagination. If there are two or three stars near the Line of Life, love affairs are likely to end in disaster.

A Star in the Triangle, if in the centre, denotes that wealth will be earned by hard work and perseverance. But if the star is near the Line of Mercury, the subject may be afflicted by loss of vision. If the star in the Triangle is at the end of a Line of Influence which comes from the Mount of Venus, it is indicative of a bereavement.

A Star in the Quadrangle suggests that the subject is controlled by his beloved. However, if under the Mounts of Saturn, Apollo, or Mercury, a very good career lies in store.

A Star on the Thumb points to numerous love affairs if the Mount of Venus is excessively developed. Two stars on the thumb may lead to the subject being overcritical of others.

A Star on the First Finger, on the first phalange, indicates that a lucky event will be the cause for a rise in the subject's position. If on the second phalange, the subject will be courageous; and if on the third phalange, immodesty may be a personality trait.

A Star on the Second Finger, on the first phalange, suggests a strong possibility of death by accident (Fig. 121). If the star is accompanied by a triangle on the Mount of Saturn, the subject may be a depraved character. If the star is on the second

---

1. The accumulation of fluid in the abdominal cavity causing swelling.

phalange, the native may be the victim of a crime; however, if it is on the third phalange, he may be a murderer himself, or be the victim of a murder.

A Star on the Third Finger, on the first phalange, denotes extraordinary brilliance in arts; if on the second phalange, the subject will possess commendable artistic talents; if on the third however, there will be an intense desire for self-praise, bordering on mania.

A Star on the Fourth Finger, on the first phalange, endows the subject with skills in public speaking; if, however, on the second phalange, the subject will be notorious for double-dealing and dishonesty (look for other negative features such as twisted fingers). A star on the third phalange is a sign of wit and humour; but if there are two stars, death may be inflicted by thieves.

A Grille

A Grille on the Mount of

Jupiter shows religious superstitions and vanity.

Saturn means that the native will not be lucky in financial matters, particularly, in old age. This sign has also been observed in the hands of convicts (Fig. 122).

Apollo denotes an inflated ego and vanity.

Mercury points to swindling and evil consequences derived therefrom (Fig. 123).

Upper Mars is a harmful sign, denoting loss of blood of the subject in an accident or fight. The subject will also have murderous tendencies.

Luna indicates that the native has an overactive imagination, resulting in obsessive neurosis, unfounded fears, anxiety phobias, or melancholia. If, however, the hand has other indications like a star on the first phalange of the third finger, or a firm hand with a strong and long Line of Apollo, the native may be able to deflect his excessive imagination towards constructive channels. If the grille is very large and covers most of the mount, it signifies numerous love affairs.

If the lower one-third part of the mount is occupied by the grille, the subject may be afflicted with kidney trouble. Such a grille in the hand of a woman denotes menstrual problems, as well as trouble with the womb and ovaries.

Venus and occupying it entirely, signifies loose morals and many love affairs.

A Grille on the Triangle is symbolic of a nervous disposition.

A Grille on the Quadrangle implies weak powers of understanding.

A Grille on the First Finger, on the first phalange, implies that the subject will live for some time in confinement in a prison, hospital, or convent. If the grille is on the second phalange, success will elude the subject, who may be tempted to take undue advantage of others. If, however, the mark is on the third phalange, imprisonment due to dishonesty and corruption may confront the native.

A Grille on the Second Finger, on the first phalange, denotes a morbid nature; if on the second phalange, diseases pertaining to the leg, loss of hearing, and the nervous system may afflict the subject. If, however, the mark is on the third phalange, miserliness will be the subject's trade mark.

A Grille on the Third Finger, on the first phalange, denotes that the native will have an inflated ego; if on the second phalange, he will have a jealous disposition; if on the third phalange, he may be poor, and hence, envious of others.

A Grille on the Fourth Finger, on the first phalange, suggests that the subject may possess dangerous tendencies of thieving and kleptomania. If the mark is on the second phalange, he may be imprisoned or face a struggle in life; a grille on the third phalange points to the subject being of a foolish disposition and given to thieving.

A Cross

A Cross on the Mount of

Jupiter is a sign of a happy marriage if the cross is formed independently. It should not be confused with an off-shoot from the Line of Life which is cut by a cross-bar

Apollo indicates lack of success (Fig. 121). If the finger of Apollo is very long, the subject will be deeply interested in heavy speculation.

Saturn will make it difficult for the subject to have children; he/she will also be prone to accidents.

Mercury is a sign that the subject's energies are channelized towards deceiving others.

Upper Mars indicates a quarrelsome nature and harmful consequences derived therefrom; it also denotes a possible injury if the mount is overdeveloped.

Luna is a sign of health problems. If in the upper part of the mount, it indicates a malfunction in the kidneys; if in the middle part, gout will bother the subject; and if in the lower part, men will suffer from kidney problems, and women from gynaecological ones.

Venus, specially if it is big, denotes ideal love.

A Cross on the Thumb signifies numerous love affairs if it is close to the nail, and the Mount of Venus is overdeveloped, or has a grille.

A Cross on the Triangle stands for a quarrelsome nature, litigation and troubles arising therefrom. Several crosses show continued ill luck. If the cross touches a major line, its effect is worse.

A Cross on the Quadrangle can have different effects, depending on its location. If it is between the Lines of Fate and Apollo, and touches the Line of Head, the subject will exert much influence over others. If it touches the Line of Fate or Apollo, it has a harmful effect on the line. If it touches the Line of Heart, the native will be influenced by the opposite sex. A big cross is called the *Mystic Cross* and signifies an aptitude for occult studies. If the cross is under the Mount of Saturn, its characteristics are religiousness and good luck.

A Cross on the First Finger, on the first phalange, is a sure sign that bad dreams, including those of death, will hound the subject; if on the upper joint of the second phalange, the cross indicates literary success and the patronage of highly-placed people. A cross on the third phalange is a sign of gluttony and excessive indulgence in worldly pleasures.

A Cross on the Second Finger, on the first phalange, points to a belief in superstitions, and criminal tendencies; if on the second phalange, there is a risk of being involved in a swindle, or an accident. A cross on the third phalange will pose impediments in having children, as well as show an inclination towards stealing.

A Cross on the Third Finger, on the first phalange, alludes to artistic tendencies, and faithfulness to the spouse. Other features such as the Lines of Heart and Influence, the Mount of Venus, and so on should also be examined. A cross on the second phalange reeks of jealousy and a highly competitive spirit; whereas one on the third phalange, unfulfillment of ambitions.

A Cross on the Fourth Finger, on the first phalange, combined with a good hand—particularly, with a good Mount and finger of Mercury—indicates success in the predictive sciences. However if the hand is bad—particularly the Mount of Mercury and the fourth finger—the subject will have an inclination towards stealing. A cross on the second phalange shows a life of struggle, and if the hand is bad, there are possibilities of conviction. A cross on the third phalange definitely points to thieving instincts and manipulation of accounts in business.

A Cross-bar

A Cross-bar on the Mount of

Jupiter indicates losses and poverty.

Saturn shows obstacles in the way of the career, particularly, in the subject's old age.

Apollo creates hurdles in the way of artistic pursuits.

Mercury, combined with a twisted finger of Mercury, denotes a check in the subject's career, and instills in him a tendency to deceive others. This fault, in turn, has negative repercussions.

Upper Mars signifies enmities.

Luna indicates a sea voyage if the bar is long; a short bar, however, damages the good effects of the mount, leading to diseases as described for the *grille* on the Mount of Luna.

Venus shows that the subject is influenced by the opposite sex.

A Cross-bar on the Thumb has different effects on each phalange. On the first phalange, it becomes a hindrance to the subject's will-power; on the second phalange, the power of logical thinking is curtailed.

A Cross-bar on the First Finger, on the first phalange, will cause the subject to believe in religious superstitions; if on the second phalange, he will be prone to jealousy, and have a tendency to deceive others. A cross-bar on the third phalange indicates a possibility of inheritance; it, however, also shows a poor digestion if the Line of Health is bad.

A Cross-bar on the Second Finger has a negative impact. If on the first phalange, it is a sign of melancholia; if the Line of Head is sloping in the direction of the Mount of Luna, the melancholia takes on the extreme form of suicidal tendencies. A bar on the second phalange indicates an obstinate nature, coupled with poor knowledge; whereas a bar on the third phalange points to an unfortunate life.

A Cross-bar on the Third Finger bars the subject from achieving success in life. More specifically, a bar on the first phalange creates obstacles in the career; one on the second phalange makes the subject inefficient and envious of others. A bar on the third phalange brings poverty and misfortune to the subject.

A Cross-bar on the Fourth Finger, on the first phalange, gives the subject the negative qualities of Mercury such as garrulousness and stealing; one on the second phalange depicts numerous career changes; and a bar on the third phalange is indicative of profit through dishonest means.

One Straight Line

One straight line on a mount or a finger has a different

meaning to numerous straight lines. The straight line in question should be vertical. Readers are by now well aware that the Lines of Fate and Apollo are vertical, while those of the Heart and Head are horizontal. While assessing the good effects of the vertical line, it should be noted that it should not be cut by any other line.

A Straight Line on the Mount of

Jupiter bestows success; however, if it lies between the Mounts of Jupiter and Saturn, it points to stomach ailments.

Saturn indicates financial prosperity.

Apollo is a sign of name, fame, and wealth.

Mercury signifies monetary gains via trade and commerce; it also highlights success in any Mercurial occupation or scientific studies.

Upper Mars stands for heroic qualities.

Luna shows that the subject has intuitive powers.

Venus denotes children (see Lines of Children, Chapter 16). Generally, several vertical lines rise from the base of the mount towards the Mount of Venus. One straight line coming towards the Line of Life should be interpreted as a Line of Influence.

A Straight Line on Each Finger, with each line covering all the three phalanges, is a warning of sudden death. To substantiate this prediction, the Lines of Life and Heart should also be looked at.

One straight line on any phalange of any finger enhances the good qualities of that finger.

Two or More Straight Lines

Straight Lines on the Mount of

Jupiter, if two in number, show that the native's ambition lies in two different spheres and his energy is diverted into two channels, thereby denying him success in either.

Saturn are an indication of success, if there are two parallel lines, one on each side of the Line of Fate. However, the presence of several lines means that success will elude the subject.

Apollo deny the subject success because he attempts numerous projects, failing to execute any. If, however, there are two lines, the talent is diverted into two channels. If one of these is the main Line of Apollo, and the other, a sister line, it is a good sign, otherwise not.

Mercury strengthen aptitude for intellectual or professional work, or for trade and commerce. If present in a female hand, the lady may marry a person endowed with the above-mentioned strengths. It should be noted that these lines should not be confused with the thin lines on the Line of Union or Marriage. The Line of Union or Marriage is horizontal, and small vertical lines on it indicate children (see Lines of Children, Chapter 16).

Upper Mars debase the subject with a brutish nature. They also produce diseases of the throat and lungs.

Luna indicate a visionary temperament. The native is not practical.

Venus are Lines of Influence and show bonds of affection. (see Lines of Influence, Chapter 14).

The principal marks on the various mounts and fingers have been explained above. Other marks should be interpreted according to the indications of the various marks discussed in the previous chapters.

Also in Orient Paperbacks

Kabala
Ancient Secrets of Numerology

Sepharial **Rs 60.00**

Kabala is an ancient work of Jewish mysticism and occult lore. Unlike other ancient systems of numerology which limit their study to the influence of numbers 0-to-9, the Jewish or the Hebrew Kabala extends the significance and interpretation of numbers to twenty-two, linking these with the twenty-two letters of the Hebrew alphabet.

In this book Sepharial explains how the knowledge of numbers. their sympathies and antipathies, discord and harmonies, can be applied in a variety of ways in our daily affairs with rewarding and profitable results.

"...explains how one can profit on speculative activities and turn the financial wheel of fortune in his favour by finding out his lucky and money numbers based on the day of the week and the hour in which one is born."

The Hindu

Also in Orient Paperbacks

Know Your Future
Through Your Date of Birth

Shiraz **Rs 60.00**

Numbers, like the holy *mantras,* wield powerful influence on all events in the universe. Each primary number from 1 to 9 is, in fact, a cosmic code having its own special characteristics, its own exclusive subjects and its own good and bad effects.

This book will teach you to interpret the unique combination of numbers in your date of birth or that of anyone else. It will help you to read a person's character, hidden nature, habits, emotional and sexual characteristics, harmonious relationships, harmful influences, etc.

Shiraz is a well-known numerologist with a large clientele.